London City Churches

Drawings: Paul Middleton
Text: Leigh Hatts

Bankside *press*

2003

First published in 2003 by Bankside Press
27 Blackfriars Road, London SE1 8NY
www.banksidepress.com

www.londoncitychurches.com

Drawings © 1992-2003 Paul Middleton
Text © 2003 Leigh Hatts

ISBN 0-9545705-0-2

A catalogue record for this book is available from the British
Library

Design and typesetting: James Hatts

Printed in the UK by The Colour Works

Contents

Map	5
Foreword	6
Introduction	8
All Hallows-by-the-Tower	10
All Hallows-on-the-Wall	12
St Andrew's Holborn	14
St Andrew Undershaft	16
St Andrew-by-the-Wardrobe	18
St Anne & St Agnes	20
St Bartholomew the Great	22
St Bartholomew the Less	24
St Benet's	26
St Botolph's Aldersgate	28
St Botolph's Aldgate	30
St Botolph's Bishopsgate	32
St Bride's Fleet Street	34
St Clement's Eastcheap	36
St Dunstan-in-the-West	38
The Dutch Church Austin Friars	40
St Edmund the King	42
St Ethelburga's	44
St Giles Cripplegate	46
St Helen's Bishopsgate	48
St James Garlickhythe	50
St Katharine Cree	52
St Lawrence Jewry	54
St Magnus the Martyr	56
St Margaret Lothbury	58
St Margaret Pattens	60
St Martin's Ludgate	62
St Mary Abchurch	64
St Mary Aldermary	66
St Mary-le-Bow	68
St Mary-at-Hill	70
St Mary Moorfields	72
St Mary Woolnoth	74

St Michael's Cornhill   76
St Michael Paternoster Royal   78
St Nicholas Cole Abbey   80
St Olave's Hart Street   82
St Peter's Cornhill   84
St Sepulchre's   86
St Stephen Walbrook   88
St Vedast   90

Church Addresses   92
Other Addresses   94
Select Bibliography   95
Index   96

Map Key

1 All Hallows-by-the-Tower
2 All Hallows-on-the-Wall
3 St Andrew's Holborn
4 St Andrew Undershaft
5 St Andrew-by-the-Wardrobe
6 St Anne & St Agnes
7 St Bartholomew the Great
8 St Bartholomew the Less
9 St Benet's
10 St Botolph's Aldersgate
11 St Botolph's Aldgate
12 St Botolph's Bishopsgate
13 St Bride's Fleet Street
14 St Clement's Eastcheap
15 St Dunstan-in-the-West
16 The Dutch Church Austin Friars
17 St Edmund the King
18 St Ethelburga's
19 St Giles Cripplegate
20 St Helen's Bishopsgate
21 St James Garlickhythe

22 St Katharine Cree
23 St Lawrence Jewry
24 St Magnus the Martyr
25 St Margaret Lothbury
26 St Margaret Pattens
27 St Martin's Ludgate
28 St Mary Abchurch
29 St Mary Aldermary
30 St Mary-le-Bow
31 St Mary-at-Hill
32 St Mary Moorfields
33 St Mary Woolnoth
34 St Michael's Cornhill
35 St Michael Paternoster Royal
36 St Nicholas Cole Abbey
37 St Olave's Hart Street
38 St Peter's Cornhill
39 St Sepulchre's
40 St Stephen Walbrook
41 St Vedast

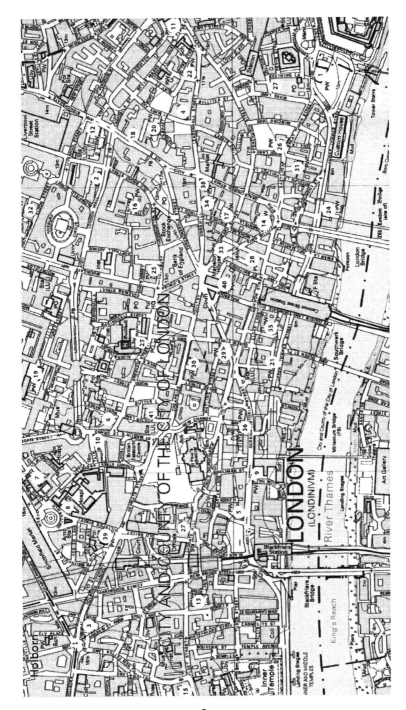

5

Foreword

That splendid leisure activity of church crawling has all but disappeared" says Philip Ursell, former Principal of Pusey House, lamenting the need for security.

However, Simon Jenkins, author of *England's Thousand Best Churches*, recently observed that "there are more insurance claims for locked churches being vandalised than for open ones".

In the City of London it is possible to spend a day church crawling because most are open. The City Churches can easily be compared to those in Cologne, Rome or Venice where people go on holiday to see the numerous historic churches.

Architectural commentator Marcus Binney says that the City Churches "constitute one of the largest and best collections of small scale architectural gems in the world". Bishop of London Richard Chartres describes them as "one of the finest ensembles of ecclesiastical buildings in Europe" and adds that he never visits a City church "without learning something new and marvelling afresh at how much there is to enjoy".

More people attend City churches for worship than many appreciate. The last two bi-annual special services for City congregations at St Paul's Cathedral, addressed by the Bishop, have seen the demand for the special service sheet outstrip an already high print run. At the Millennium the City Churches were recording the highest growth in church service attendance in the country.

The present surge of interest and activity in the City Churches is largely the result of Archbishop David Hope's short period as Bishop of London. In 1992 he established the City Churches Commission, under the chairmanship of Lord Templeman, to examine the future of the churches. Two years later the Templeman Report suggested that 27 churches could be considered for redundancy and conversion for another use.

Although the controversial proposals were never implemented, the uproar and debate which followed publication led not only to the re-establishment of the now very active Friends of the the City Churches but also to a reassessment by each church of its role and mission.

In 1998 the City Churches Development Group was set up to increase public access to the City Churches, especially those which were finding it difficult to open on a daily basis.

The Templeman Report also led to the City Corporation and English Heritage funding a complete photographic record of the churches by the Royal Commission on the Historical Monuments of England.

In 1994 the City had about 5000 residents but this figure has now grown. There are also about 280,000 daytime inhabitants. Most are under forty and well off. But as the Square Mile is one of the world's three leading financial centres they are often stressed and tired. They spend more hours in the City than at home and so are more likely to worship and be involved in a City Church than at their parish church in the suburbs or Home Counties.

Just as the Corporation of London's responsibilities extend far beyond the City boundaries so does the fame and ministry of the City Churches where the offices of such bodies as Christian Aid, Greenbelt and the Mission to Seafarers can be found. Bishop Chartres has described the parishes as having "a mobile working population with tentacles which stretch all over the globe".

The average age of City clergy is, like the congregations, getting younger so that there is now a mixture of energy and experience in a team which is working in a more collegial manner than in the last century.

In 1250 the City had a hundred parishes and 13 monasteries. After the Great Fire in 1666 only 21 of the 108 churches remained intact. By 1670 it was agreed that 51 should be rebuilt with the commission going to Christopher Wren who was assisted by his colleague and fellow scientist Robert Hooke. Today 23 Wren churches survive after Victorian rationalisation and the Second World War.

In 1994 St Mary Moorfields, the Roman Catholic church which was once a pro-cathedral, became a City church when the City boundary was moved to embrace the building.

David Hope's successor as Bishop of London can now, a decade after the Templeman Report, speak of "a recovery of confidence in the future of the City Churches as centres of imaginative Christian work in the Square Mile".

Leigh Hatts

Introduction

I t all began when I moved to Spitalfields in 1990. I was fascinated by the energy and life there as well as the many characters and buildings. I was often asked why I lived there. Later on people realised that it was "an interesting area". Of special interest was the area around the fruit and vegetable market with Hawksmoor's masterpiece Christchurch just across the road. I was encouraged to do a number of drawings in this area which later formed the basis of a small show in a local architect's office. The drawings reproduced well and were later made available as a set of cards.

Living on the edge of the City of London and as a practising architect (in community/educational, cultural buildings and conservation), I have always had an interest in the City Churches. At the time the total was 39 (comprising 22 Wren, 8 medieval and 9 by others) now extended to 41 following City boundary changes. I was inspired to find out more and as architectural work at this time was rather quiet I spent time exploring these jewels on foot. To my pleasant surprise most of them were open and I spent a lot of time soaking up their quietness. I noted that the promotional and display material varied. To me it seemed that the churches functioned on a number of levels having religious, cultural and historical significance. They mean something different to each person.

Later on my intention was to get to know them, find out all I could about them and then to capture their quality or "atmosphere" in a series of drawings. Having many times walked around all of them I set myself the task to do just one drawing of each church. This would be an exterior or interior view which best represented each one. These were later exhibited for several weeks in St Giles Cripplegate in the Barbican in 1993. Looking back I think that I must have been influenced by the work of Dennis Creffield and his English Cathedrals exhibition at the South Bank Centre. As well as this, Geoffrey Fletcher's illustrations of London captured the richness of the ordinary everyday things going on in cities.

As to my actual drawing style, the person I look to most is Paul Hogarth and his books *Drawing Architecture* and *Drawing on Life* and his exhibitions. He has spent a lifetime drawing what he sees around him. I admire him greatly and his craft as well as the humour of his drawings.

Out of my exhibition the City Churches Walk was founded in 1994 together with Christopher Fuke and Leigh Hatts. Over the previous year we met regularly and liaised with the Area Dean. The uncertainty over the future of the City Churches (where many alternative uses were being looked at) convinced us that this was a crucial and important thing to do. The annual event is now organised by the Friends of the City Churches.

On the actual day we positioned ourselves in front of St Paul's Cathedral (everyone would know where that was) and directed those who arrived to the nearby St Andrew-by-the-Wardrobe. Over 400 from near and far turned out! Lord and Lady Kennet who have a strong interest and knowledge of London churches opened the event. All those gathered were given a "passport" to be stamped as each church was visited. There was no official route although we tried to spread such a large number over all 38 churches. Each church which opened relied on its own volunteers to act as unofficial guides. Some provided refreshments. Remember that this was at a time when some churches with an uncertain future were not open regularly. We wanted to raise their public profile. Everyone who registered for the event later received a limited edition card set of the drawings. A number of these later featured in *City Events* magazine.

I have travelled widely around the world making drawings as I go I now consider myself as a London Scot. I have had several exhibitions related to the City and its edges. In 1997 I qualified as a City of London guide. My travels to India to research sacred space in different religious traditions have built on my experience of the sacred first discovered in my City church explorations. It even resulted in my designing an ecumenical chapel in Bangalore.

A special thank you to Leigh Hatts for the informative text and Bankside Press. Having tried over a long period to get the drawings published in the mainstream press I was told on many occasions that the work was too specialist and small. Hopefully we have found a gap in the market which needed to be filled.

Paul Middleton

All Hallows-by-the-Tower

The church, founded by Barking Abbey in 675, was All Hallows Berkyngechirche by the Tower which became All Hallows Barking by the Tower. It was Tubby Clayton, Toc H founder and vicar from 1922 to 1963, who dropped Barking.

The tower was rebuilt in 1659, a rare case of a church being improved during the Cromwellian years, and it was from there that seven years later Samuel Pepys watched the Great Fire. Admiral Penn, father of Pennsylvania founder William, saved the church by having houses pulled down to halt the flames.

But in 1940 bombs caused massive destruction. The church was rededicated in 1957 after restoration by Lord Mottistone who was able to reveal a Saxon arch made with Roman tiles.

The church's interior is surprisingly large and light. Part of a 15th-century Flemish altarpiece survives and a large number of brasses. The statues of St James the Great and St Roch are 500 years old. The pulpit comes from the lost St Swithin's London Stone. The old font was carved by Second World War Sicilian prisoners and has a delightful wooden cover carved in 1682 by Grinling Gibbons.

Baptised here were Bishop Lancelot Andrewes and William Penn. Weddings include Judge Jeffreys and future US President John Quincy Adams. Being near the Tower there were burials of headless bodies including St John Fisher who is commemorated by a 1999 icon triptych by Michael Coles.

The main entrance was on the south side until Byward Street was built in the 1880s but a James Gibbs-style south entry with an automatic door created in 2002 gives access from the new Tower Place square. Also new is the Vestry restaurant in a walled garden.

This, the church of HM Customs & Excise, has the Archdeacon of London as Vicar and a strong Sunday congregation with a Sunday School. Beating the Bounds on Ascension Day involves a boat trip to the parish boundary and sometimes a clash with Beefeaters beating the Tower's Liberty. The Toc H lamp burns as a symbol of the Light of Christ and the international ministry here embraces the Friends of the Diocese of Cyprus and the Gulf.

Paul Middleton

All Hallows-on-the-Wall

The first mention of the church is 1108 when Queen Matilda, wife of Henry I, endowed the church whose north wall stands on the foundations of London's Roman wall. In 1471 a cell was added for anchorite Simon the Anker who spent twenty years writing *The Fruyte of Redemcyon* which was printed in 1514 by Wynkn de Worde on his press next to St Bride's.

Statesman Sir Francis Knollys married his second wife Lettice here in the year of the Spanish Armada threat 1588.

Although the church survived the 1666 Great Fire of London it was rebuilt a century later. It is George Dance the Younger's very first building and he always referred to it as "my first child". He was just 24 years old and much influenced by the architecture of Rome.

The small church, raised on a crypt, has no aisles and the pulpit can only be entered from the vestry. The painting behind the altar, *St Paul receiving his sight from Ananias* by Dance's brother Nathaniel Dance-Holland, is a copy of Pietro da Cortona's painting in Santa Maria della Concezione in Rome.

Just over a century ago the Rector was JS Stone who wrote the hymn *The Church's One Foundation* often sung during the Week of Prayer for Christian Unity. This is appropriate for Christians of many traditions are drawn here to Christian Aid's London and South-East headquarters with its slogan 'We believe in life before death'. Also here is the Amos Trust, working with peacemakers in the Holy Land and elsewhere, and the team organising the annual Greenbelt festival on Cheltenham racecourse.

The priest-in-charge is the singer-song writer Garth Hewitt who has written a song about the City Churches. The one regular service is Wednesday on the Wall at 6.30pm which Garth Hewitt describes as "a time to pause, find inspiration and pray". At lunchtime on the last Friday of the month there is a talk about Christian Aid's work.

JS Stone's rectory was replaced in 1902 by the adjoining hall which was built as a shelter for commuters who, arriving at Liverpool Street Station on early morning cheap tickets, needed somewhere to wait before work began.

Paul Middleton

St Andrew's Holborn

The first mention of St Andrew's is in 951 when the church was a wooden building at the top of the hill above the River Fleet. During Norman times it was called St Andrew Holburnestrate and by 1291 it was St Andrew de Holeburn.

The church survived the Great Fire because the wind changed just at the last moment but it was rebuilt anyway by Wren. However, the 15th-century tower was retained and escaped the bomb which destroyed the nave in 1941.

Today's building opened in 1961 with furnishings from the Foundling Hospital Chapel in Coram's Fields. Captain Thomas Coram, who is buried here, set up the hospital with help from artist William Hogarth and composer George Handel who gave recitals to raise money.

The Royal Free Hospital owes its foundation to local doctor William Marsden who discovered a young girl dying on the church steps and was unable to find her a bed.

Weddings include Lord Chief Justice Coke who in 1598 married 'the Lady of Bleeding Heart Yard', Sir Christopher Hatton's widow. In 1799 engineer Marc Brunel married Sophia Kingdom whose son was railway pioneer Isambard Kingdom Brunel. In 1808 Charles Lamb was best man and his sister Mary bridesmaid at the wedding of essayist William Hazlitt. Two prime ministers – Henry Addington and Benjamin Disraeli – were christened here .

The church was at the top of steps until 1869 but is now at the bottom due to the raising of the road for the Holborn Viaduct. The loss of the churchyard resulted in 12,000 bodies being removed to Manor Park and in 2002 a further 2,700 bodies were exhumed from the crypt. So tragic poet Thomas Chatterton, who died in 1770, now lies near Ilford.

The church is the headquarters of the Royal College of Organists so there are plenty of recitals. St Andrew's models itself on St Gervais in Paris by attempting to bring contemplation to the world of work. Liturgy is the heart of the mission and hospitality part of the discipline so the cleared crypt is to be a restaurant

Paul Middleton

St Andrew Undershaft

The church, mentioned in the 12th century, was called St Andrew-juxta-Aldgate and St Andrew Cornhill but then Undershaft took hold from the 15th-century because of a tall maypole erected outside every May Day. During the rest of the year the pole hung under the eaves of houses in Shaft Alley but in 1549 it was destroyed after a fiery preacher denounced it as "heathen".

The church was rebuilt in its present form in about 1530 during Henry VIII's reign. The roof bosses include Henry's rose and Katharine of Aragon's pomegranate.

The font was made in 1634 by Nicholas Stone, Charles I's master mason, for £16. The pulpit is late 17th-century. The outstanding organ case was built in 1695 but in 1858 it was moved into the tight corner on the south side.

The west window was shattered by the IRA bomb which exploded outside the nearby Baltic Exchange late one night in 1992. The replacement reflects the old by including the names of all monarchs from Edward VI to William III except for the Roman Catholic Mary and James II. However the 16th-century heraldic glass fragments in the aisle windows survived.

A plaque commemorates the painter Hans Holbein who lived in the parish. The oldest brass is the 1539 memorial to Sheriff of London Nicholas Leveson and his wife Dionysia who was the daughter of Thomas Bodley, founder of Oxford's Bodleian Library.

The John Stow memorial was erected by his widow and restored by the Merchant Taylors' Company in 1905 on the 300th anniversary of his death. Stow, author of *Stow's Survey of London* which is the first complete City Churches record, is depicted writing at a desk. The real quill pen is renewed by the Lord Mayor during the Stow Commemoration Service.

In 1898 Charles Turner became both Rector and the one and only Bishop of Islington.

In the 21st century the church is an annex to St Helen's and under the shaft of Norman Foster's Swiss Re 'Gherkin'

Paul Middleton

St Andrew-by-the-Wardrobe

In 1244 this was St Andrea de Castello which is a reference to Baynard's Castle – now recalled only by the next door pub. The earliest use of the name St Andrew-by-the-Wardrobe is 1361 when the King's Wardrobe, now Wardrobe Place, was built on the north side for the state robes. Parishioner William Shakespeare, who is commemorated in the church, visited the Wardrobe to collect material for costumes and his Players were fitted out there with their uniforms for James I's Coronation procession.

After the Great Fire only the church was rebuilt. This was the last and cheapest of Wren's churches when completed in 1695.

St Andrew's stands on high ground above Puddle Dock but until the building of Queen Victoria Street in 1871 there was a churchyard on the south side rather than the very steep climb up to the south door.

In the 1920s the church was known to future Foreign Secretary George Brown who as a boy was a server here. Familiar figures at the time included Windsor's Clewer nuns who had their London house across the river. In 1940 an incendiary bomb destroyed the church interior leaving only the walls and the tower.

Today's building was completed in 1961 to the design of Marshall Sisson who used Wren's plans. The plain west window comes from Bulstrode Park House in Buckinghamshire.

Appropriately, for a church where members of the Society of King Charles the Martyr hold services, the Royal Arms are Stuart. The church, which now embraces neighbouring St Ann's parish, has an Italian 16th-century wooden figure of St Ann holding the Virgin holding the Child. High up on the stairs is the St Nicholas figure from the gate of St Nicholas Cole Abbey. A memorial window to MP and author Ivor Bulmer-Thomas, who was churchwarden for 37 years until 1993, features the churches he helped to save including St John's Smith Square.

This was the parish church of *The Times* with the words "Printed and published in the parish of St Andrew-by-the-Wardrobe" appearing daily on the back page until the paper moved in 1974.

Paul Middleton

St Anne & St Agnes

The dedication of the City's Lutheran Church to Anne and Agnes, Mary's mother and the Roman virgin martyr, is unique and the reason is a mystery. The church, which existed in the early 12th century, has been called St Agnes-near-Alderychgate, St Anne-near-Aldersgate, St Anne-in-the-Willows and by 1467 St Anne and St Agnes-within-Aldrichesgate.

The old building was lost in a fire in 1548 and the replacement destroyed in the Great Fire. This was within living memory of the vicar being executed for objecting to Charles I's execution.

The present small brick building is by Wren although Hooke may have had a hand as it is known that he visited the site more than once.

John Wesley preached twice in 1738 which was the year of his 'conversion'. In 1933 the first Bishop of Fulham, Dr Basil Batty, became Rector whilst continuing to have responsibility for Anglican churches in northern and central Europe.

Following Second World War damage the City served the church with a Dangerous Structure Notice which was ignored by the Verger who insisted on opening the church. Prior to the bombing the church had only been just visible between other buildings.

With peace consideration was given to converting it into the Bishop of London's residence. Instead in 1966 the church became home to the Lutheran congregation which has restored it to as near as Wren would have known it. Furnishings are from several lost City Churches including St Michael Wood Street, St Augustine Watling Street and St Mildred Bread Street. The beautiful plaster ceiling is appreciated by many who attend the lunchtime concerts.

St Anne & St Agnes is well known for its music. Bach Vespers can only be heard regularly in three places – New York, Leipzig and St Anne & St Agnes. Also popular is the monthly Sunday night Jazz Vespers and the Bach Cantata series. Based here, and providing much of the music, is the Lecosaldi Ensemble, a group of professional musicians directed by composer Peter Lea-Cox. There are Swahili, Estonian and Latvian language services as well as English.

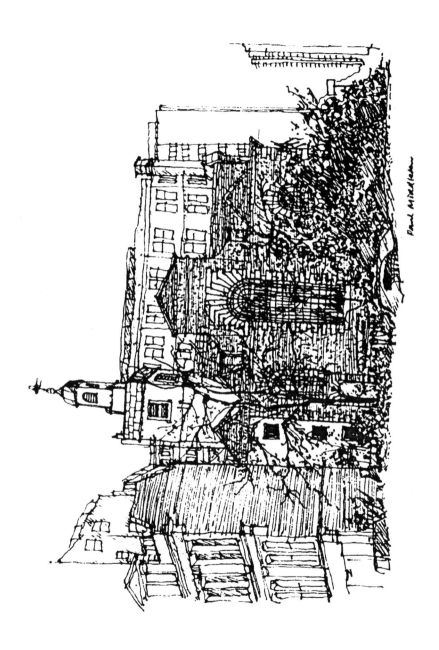

St Bartholomew the Great

This is a priory church founded in 1123 by Rahere, Henry I's jester, in thanksgiving for being cured in Rome's Ospedale San Bartolomeo. He was the prior and the monks' main work was running a similar hospital which continues now as Bart's.

When the Augustinian community was dissolved in 1539 the nave was demolished forcing the congregation to sit even today collegiate-style in the choir. Later the Lady Chapel became a print works where US founding father Benjamin Franklin was an apprentice. Artist William Hogarth was baptised here.

Today's church is the result of restoration in the 1890s by Sir Aston Webb, the churchwarden's brother. There is a superb choir and a high standard of liturgy worthy of the building where the founder's tomb stands prominently by the high altar.

Annual events include the St Luke's-tide hospital service, the Butchers' Company service and St Bartholomew's Day Solemn Eucharist when sheep are blessed in church. On Good Friday the clergy and choir gather outdoors on the former nave site for the Butterworth Charity service when hot cross buns are distributed. After decimalisation Rector Arthur Brown kept an old 6d in his cassock pocket just in case a parish widow claimed the ancient dole. The most atmospheric service is the candlelit Easter Vigil which begins with the lighting of the fire in the cloister.

The Christmas Bazaar, on Lord Mayor's Show Day, is noted for a book sale in the choir stalls and cakes in the ambulatory.

The great 20th-century incumbent was Newall Wallbank who came in 1937 as a curate, was Rector from 1945 until 1979 and died during evensong here in 1996. As curate he ran the parish whilst Rector Canon Edwin Savage, his godfather, lived in Eastbourne during the week. He usually started out for the train during Sunday evensong leaving Wallbank to conclude the service.

This was the first City Church to have its web address on the church banner and the first to have the Euro symbol on the collecting box. This much filmed church is the fifth church in *Four Weddings and A Funeral*.

Paul Middleton

St Bartholomew the Less

This small church is just inside the St Bartholomew's Hospital gatehouse. Above the archway is London's only statue of Henry VIII who in 1536 closed down St Bartholomew's Priory which ran the hospital. But within a decade he reopened the hospital turning its Holy Cross Chapel, dating from about 1184, into St Bartholomew the Less to distinguish it from the Great. He also made it a parish church with the boundary being the hospital walls so unusually the hospital chaplain is an incumbent and the chapel has churchwardens and a parochial church council.

The square tower, which peeps over the hospital wall, and the vestry are 15th-century but the church has twice been rebuilt since Tudor times. In 1789 George Dance the Younger designed the present octagon plan first built in wood and copied in stone by Thomas Hardwick just 34 years later. His grandson made further alterations in 1862-4.

Second World War damage resulted in further restoration work but the building continues to offer a contrast to James Gibbs' 18th-century hospital building.

Post-war restoration included stained glass by Hugh Easton whose west windows depict St Luke, who was a doctor, and St Bartholomew with his arm around hospital founder Rahere.

This constant rebuilding has resulted in a high level floor but the vestibule has its original stone floor. Two of the four bells are 15th-century.

There are numerous memorials to many staff associated with this chapel which sees medical weddings, funerals and memorial services. In the vestry there is a 16th-century altar tomb of Elizabeth Freke and her surgeon husband John. But in the north-east corner of the church a surprise memorial recalls Thomas Bodley, founder of Oxford's Bodleian Library, and his wife Anne who lived in the hospital precinct. Architect Inigo Jones, son of a Smithfield clothworker, was baptised here in 1573.

This is an ecumenical ministry with the lunchtime Mass being Anglican or Roman Catholic.

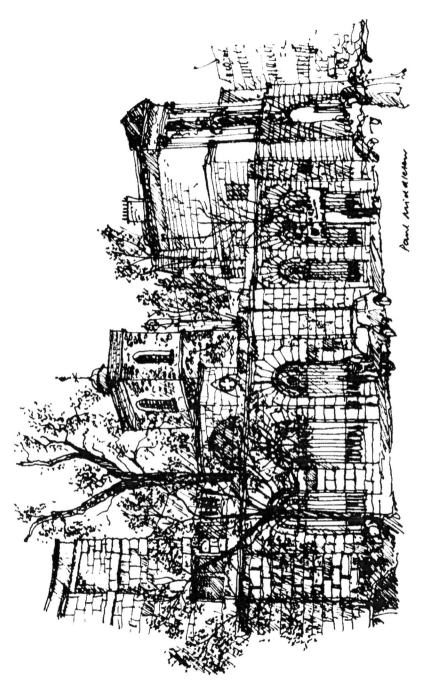

St Benet's

In 1111 this was known as St Benedict-above-the-Thames and by Elizabeth I's reign St Benet Hithe. Shakespeare's *Twelfth Night* calls the pre-Fire church St Bennet.

Although surrounded by fast roads with no direct access to the Thames this is often still called St Benet's Paul's Wharf. The name recalls the time when stone was landed from the river for the new cathedral designed by Wren who was also at least partly responsible for St Benet's. However, its Dutch feel suggests that Hooke may have had a hand. The little church was completed in 1683 and includes Portland stone which never made it up to the cathedral.

A plaque recalls London-born Welshman Inigo Jones, who gave generously to the old church where he was buried. There is a medallion bust of Sir Robert Wyseman, Dean of the Court of Arches and a St Benet's benefactor, who knew both churches.

The present building saw the wedding in 1747 of novelist Henry Fielding to his wife's maid.

This became the Welsh Church in 1879 when the Welsh Anglicans had to leave St Etheldreda's in Ely Place which was being returned to the Roman Catholic Church. The services, which are in Welsh, now attract only a modest number giving it the air of a Welsh country church. But many exiled members of the Church in Wales come for annual events such as the National Welsh Festival, harvest festival and the Bilingual Carol Service in Advent which are all followed by a Welsh tea.

With the College of Arms nearby there has been a long association with the Heralds. A 1688 monument commemorates Gregory King who was Rouge Dragon Pursuivant. A Somerset Herald remembered with a plaque is John Charles Brook who died in 1797 when the ceiling of the Haymarket Theatre collapsed.

When Garter King of Arms Sir Anthony Wagner died in 1995 the church saw the first heraldic funeral since the 18th century with officers wearing their tabards. The last vicar was Alfred Pryse-Hawkins who as a St Woolos Cathedral canon was able to place a canon's hat above his own arms.

Paul Middleton

St Botolph's Aldersgate

The church of St Botolph-without-Aldersgate, once St Botulph without Ailredesgate, existed in 1086 when William I confirmed the nearby St Martin-le-Grand Priory as the patron. Botolph was a 7th-century Saxon abbot who became the patron of travellers giving his name to other City gateway churches. It was the position of the church just outside the wall which protected it from the Great Fire. Only the north wall needed repair. However, the church now, although standing on pre-Fire foundations, is mainly Georgian having been rebuilt with a barrel-vaulted roof and bell-turret in 1778-91.

The eastern facade with its Venetian window was added in 1831 when the chancel had eight feet lopped off to allow for the widening of Aldersgate Street. This improved the approach to the General Post Office and today the churchyard, embracing those of Christ Church Newgate and St Leonard's Foster Lane, is still known as Postman's Park. In the park is the Watts' Cloister, built at the expense of artist GF Watts, to commemorate unsung heroes. Inscriptions include 'Thomas Simpson died of exhaustion after saving many lives by breaking ice at Highgate Ponds, Jan 25 1885' and 'Daniel Pemberton, aged 61, foreman LSWR, surprised by a train when gauging the line, hurled his mate out of the track, saving his life at the cost of his own'. Michael Ayrton's bronze Minotaur was added to the garden in 1973. The view from here of the church, with headstones stacked against the south wall, contrasts with the barrack-like exterior in the narrow street known as Little Britain.

The church, which nearly became a postal museum in 1979, was restored during the 1990s. There is a blue and gold apse and the mahogany pulpit rests on a palm tree. Many monuments come from the old church including Lady Anne Packington's table-tomb dated 1563. The east window is a painting on glass completed in 1788 by James Pearson showing the Agony in the Garden. Three windows in the south gallery came from St Matthew's Spring Gardens when it was demolished in 1885.

St Botolph is the church of the Ironmongers and the Plaisterers.

Pencil Animal Kebar

St Botolph's Aldgate

The church, which belonged to a priory just inside the wall, existed in Saxon times. Aldgate comes from Old Gate and, as the church stood just outside the City gateway, its full name is St Botolph-without-Aldgate.

Although the church escaped the Great Fire it was rebuilt in 1744 to a design by George Dance the Elder who had just finished Mansion House. The Portland stone spire and domed entrances flanking the main door owe much to Wren's influence. Retained is a memorial to Lord Darcy and Sir Nicholas Carew who were executed by Henry VIII and buried in the old church. The new church was improved in the 1880s with the ceiling decorated with shield-carrying angels by John Francis Bentley who was to become famous for Westminster Cathedral.

Daniel Defoe was married here in 1683 and Jeremy Bentham was one of the first to be christened in the present building. Rectors include Thomas Bray who founded the SPCK and USPG.

In the Second World War a bomb landed on the church without exploding. The last restoration, following a fire, was by Rodney Tatchell and the re-opening in 1966 was attended by the Queen Mother. George Appleton, who became Bishop in Jerusalem, opened the crypt to homeless people and began the outreach which caused John Betjeman to observe that St Botolph's was "more a mission to the east end than a City church". In the 1970s a weekly disco in the crypt regularly ran until 2.30am.

Once the parish was mainly Jewish and the London Diocesan Council for Christian-Jewish Understanding is based here. Now nearby residents are mainly Muslim and the church has become a bridge across the parish boundary between the wealth of the City and poverty of the most Britain's populous ward in Tower Hamlets. Clergy include Ken Leech who holds the post, unique in the City, of Community Theologian focusing on the East End.

At the Sir John Cass's Foundation service pupils of many cultures wear a red feather recalling the founder's death in 1718 when he suffered a haemorrhage whilst signing his will.

Paul Middleton

St Botolph's Bishopsgate

The name St Botolph-without-Bishopsgate indicates that the church is just outside the City wall. The earliest mention is in 1212 as Sci botulfi exa bissopeg.

In 1571 the ancient church was rebuilt at the expense of Lord Mayor Sir William Allen. This survived the Great Fire but the Elizabethan building was still demolished in 1724 and the present brick building opened on the site in 1728. Architect James Gould, assisted by his son-in-law George Dance the Elder, broke with convention and placed the stone tower at the east end on Bishopsgate. The public had to enter on each side of the high altar unlike today when the main entrance is the south doorway from the garden added by John Francis Bentley in 1892.

There have been at least eight restorations. The insertion of a dome and lantern in 1828 brightened the interior. The chancel under the tower, giving the church a feeling of length, was remodelled in 1878.

At the base of the gallery are the names of incumbents since 1323 including Alfred Earle who from 1896 to 1900 was simultaneously the Bishop of Marlborough. Successors were sometimes either also Bishops of Kensington or Willesden including Gerald Ellison who later became Bishop of London.

Baptisms include Edward Alleyn, friend of Shakespeare and founder of Dulwich College, in the old church and poet John Keats in the present building. A tablet recalls Sir Paul Pindar, buried here in 1650, whose house facade is preserved in the Victoria & Albert Museum.

The church was badly damaged by the IRA bomb which devastated Bishopsgate in 1993. In the following months rector Alan Tanner continued the regular celebration of the Eucharist although he and the congregation had to wear hard hats. The thanksgiving service for restoration took place in 1997.

In the churchyard there is a restaurant built in 1894 as a Turkish bath but with an entrance based on the outer casing of Christ's tomb in the Holy Sepulchre.

Paul Middleton

St Bride's Fleet Street

S t Bridget, or Bride, built her church here on a Roman brick foundation. The Norman rebuild was used for a meeting of a parliament in King John's reign. Wynkyn de Worde, Caxton's apprentice, assembled his press next to St Bride's in 1500 because he knew that influential Church communicators were here. The Bishop of Salisbury was nearby and the Abbot of Peterborough was on the future site of the *Telegraph* – hence the paper's long-running Peterborough column. In the 17th century the growing number of printing presses attracted writers such as Dryden, Evelyn and Milton to the parish. Diarist Samuel Pepys and his eight brothers and sisters were all baptised here. He records bribing the gravedigger with sixpence to "justle together" the bodies in the crypt to make room for his brother Tom. Soon the Great Plague killed 238 parishioners in a week and then the Great Fire destroyed the church.

Wren's replacement was his most expensive. The steeple, the model for the now traditional wedding cake first made by a baker on Ludgate Hill, was added in 1703 and survived 1940 bombing. The church was rebuilt within the Wren walls with help from newspapers as indicated by plaques on the collegiate-style seats.

Exiled Fleet Street reassembles here for weddings and funerals. The Bishop of London calls it the "cathedral of communication". When the *Daily Express* killed off the William Hickey diary it was at the St Bride's doorway that *Mail* rival Nigel Dempster staged a mock funeral.

The church has a reproduction of the first edition of the *Daily Courant*, the first newspaper. In the crypt, where the Eucharist is celebrated daily, visitors can see the *Evening News* report of the bombing of St Bride's.

The choral services are sung by a professional choir costing £100,000 a year. The repertoire includes the Bubble anthem sung at the Stationers' annual Bubble Sermon service. Agricultural journalists organise the harvest festival which is followed by an auction of fruit, vegetables and honey. But the high point of the year is the dawn Easter Eucharist followed by egg rolling down Fleet Street.

ST. BRIDES CHURCH   Paul Middleton © May 1993

St Clement's Eastcheap

The church in Clements Lane, first mentioned in 1067, was in the 13th century known as St Clement-by-Kandelwikstrete. The church is still in Candlewick Ward but the present name is a reminder that, before King William Street was built in 1838, Eastcheap ran further west to Clements Lane.

The church, much rebuilt in 1632, was one of the first to be destroyed in the Great Fire. The Wren replacement, completed in 1687, is oblong with the south side tapering inwards from the south-west tower. The west wall was moved a few feet back to widen Clements Lane and fourteen feet was added at the east end in compensation as the church also had to accommodate the congregation from the destroyed St Martin Orgar.

In 1872 William Butterfield reordered the interior by raising the sanctuary, dividing the altarpiece, removing a gallery and filling the plain windows with stained glass. An admirer of the church in the late 19th century was William Gladstone who was much taken with the gilded flames on the font cover then always on display. In 1933 Sir Ninian Comper reassembled the altarpiece and employed W Butchart to paint Clement crowned as Pope. Three years later the organ was restored to its original position above the entrance.

Bomb damage in 1940 led to most windows reverting to clear glass. The large 17th-century pulpit is made of Norwegian oak and has impressive swags and cherubs.

This is the original Oranges and Lemons Church. The famous annual service at St Clement Danes only started in 1920 and most churches in the nursery rhyme are within the Square Mile. Indeed Spanish oranges were regularly landed on a nearby quay.

The church, which houses the National Interpreting Service working 24 hours with the emergency services, has a weekly lunchtime celebration of the Eucharist on Wednesday. In December the raised sanctuary provides a stage for medieval mystery plays by the Players of St Peter who were formed in 1946 at St Peter's Cornhill. A year round second hand bargain book sale at the back offers interesting titles.

Paul Middleton

St Dunstan-in-the-West

The first mention of this church is in 1185 although the dedication suggests a date of around 1025 before the Normans arrived. St Dunstan-over-against-the-New-Temple became St Dunstan-in-the-West when St Dunstan-near-the-Tower began to be called St Dunstan-in-the-East in the 1280s.

Bible translator William Tyndale was a curate and Rectors include Sion College founder Thomas White who was followed by poet John Donne. Izaac Walton was a sidesman when his *Compleat Angler* was published in the churchyard. Lord Baltimore, who gave his name to Baltimore in the USA, was buried in the old church. The Earl of Strafford, impeached and executed under Charles I, was baptised here. Praisegod Barebones, who gave his name to Cromwell's Barebones Parliament, was married here. In the same century Samuel Pepys found pretty women in the congregation a distraction from the sermon.

Thanks to the Dean of Westminster, who roused the Abbey schoolboys in the middle of night to bring buckets, the Great Fire just missed the church which survived until 1829 when the widening of Fleet Street led to demolition.

The present building has a lantern tower inspired by the tower of All Saints Pavement in York which was lit at night to guide travellers in the nearby forest. The clock, with two giants striking the hours, was part of the old church and added in 1671 as a thanksgiving for escape from the Fire. Press baron Lord Rothermere brought the clock back to the new church in 1936. Below is a memorial to his brother and *Daily Mail* founder Lord Northcliffe. Less prominent is a plaque to JL Garvin who edited *The Observer* for 34 years. The statue of Elizabeth I is from Lud Gate and is not only the oldest public statue of a monarch but has its own maintenance fund.

The church is both Anglican and Romanian Orthodox as a result of Archbishop Michael Ramsey's visit to Romania in 1965. The compact octagon is the most extraordinary of any City church interior allowing for both the Anglican high altar as well as the Orthodox iconostasis (screen) from Bucharest.

Paul Middleton

The Dutch Church Austin Friars

The name Austin Friars recalls that this was a priory church of the Augustinian friars. Henry III's Constable Humphry de Bohun founded it on his return from a crusade in 1253. The site ran north to London Wall and west as far as Copthall Avenue and was important enough to be attacked in 1381 during the Peasants' Revolt. Wat Tyler's men murdered thirteen people who had sought sanctuary. The Black Prince's son Edward was buried here as were many barons who died at the Battle of Barnet which ended of the Wars of the Roses. The monks also often received the bodies of those executed at Tower Hill.

In 1513 it was a lodging for Dutch scholar Erasmus who thought the wine to be rather poor quality. Augustinian Miles Coverdale stayed briefly when working on his translation of the Bible.

At the Dissolution the domestic buildings were turned into a residence by the Marquess of Winchester who had already taken Netley Abbey in Hampshire as his country house. He is remembered by Great Winchester Street at the end of Austin Friars Passage.

In 1550 Edward VI gave the church to Dutch Protestant refugees and, apart from the brief period of Mary I's reign, it has been the Dutch Church ever since. It just missed being enveloped by the Great Fire but in 1940 a bomb completely destroyed the old building. Pictures of the old church include a Van Gogh sketch.

On the 400th anniversary of Edward VI's gift, 10 year old Princess Irene of Holland who had been a wartime member of the congregation laid the foundation stone of the new church. The building by Arthur Bailey opened in 1954 with just a fragment of old stonework outside. Inside and below the Communion Table is the damaged altar stone from the original church. The Dutch-built organ is unique to Britain. The stained glass windows depict Edward VI, Dutch William of Orange and his English wife Mary and Princess Irene. Outside on the wall is the cypher of George VI along with those of Queen Wilhelmina and Queen Juliana.

On Sundays the 11am service is in Dutch with strong Dutch coffee served in the social hall afterwards.

St Edmund the King

The Lombard Street church, like the neighbouring banks with their hanging signs, opens on to the street and also has a clock projecting over the pavement. St Edmund the King, often called just St Edmund King, was founded about 1000 – about 170 years after King Edmund of East Anglia was killed by the Danes. But it was first called St Edmund Grasschurch due to the hay market.

The building has always been orientated north–south and, after the Great Fire, Wren did not seek to change the alignment and left much of the plan to Hooke whose design had the personal approval of Charles II. However, thirty years later Hawksmoor had to produce a new tower and steeple after defects were reported. His final touch was twelve flaming urns which were removed around 1900. John Betjeman later suggested fibreglass replacements and there are now plans for their restoration.

The church interior, once likened to the private chapel of a nobleman's house, was twice reordered in the 19th century and suffered damage in both World Wars. But much remains including churchwardens' pews at the back and a reredos with paintings of Moses and Aaron added by William Etty in 1833.

The huge window behind the altar was made in Munich during the 1860s for St Paul's Cathedral who diverted it to St Bartholomew Moor Lane. When that church was demolished in 1902 the window was brought here as a memorial to the Duke of Clarence. Royal funeral hatchments include those of Princess Charlotte, daughter of the Prince Regent. A tablet records the death of Titanic victim Charles Melville Hays.

Rectors include Geoffrey Studdert-Kennedy who when he was appointed here in 1921 was already known as Woodbine Willie from his time as an army chaplain. Weddings include poet Joseph Addison to the Countess of Warwick in 1716.

The last baptism was in 1983 just before the robed choir was disbanded. Millennium Renewal sees the church becoming the London Centre for Spirituality with a library and bookshop.

Paul Middleton

St Ethelburga's

The dedication to Ethelburga, first Abbess of Barking and sister of Bishop of London St Erkenwald, is unique. The City's smallest church was founded in 1250 as St Adelburga's and rebuilt in 1400.

The church survived the Great Fire and the Blitz to be described by Sir John Betjeman as the best example of a medieval parish church in the City. All this was largely destroyed in 1993 by the IRA bomb which exploded outside.

Rectors include Blessed John Larke whose friend and fellow martyr St Thomas More was a parishioner; Luke Milburne, who was attacked in print by Alexander Pope for criticising John Dryden, and JM Rodwell, an early leading Anglo-Catholic, who in the 19th century gave the church a high profile.

In 1607 Henry Hudson, of Hudson River fame, and his crew received Holy Communion here before setting sail.

Until Bishopsgate was widened in 1932 there was a narrow building in front of the church so one entered through a porch with tiny shops on either side. The revealed Kentish ragstone west front with the central door and bell turret were destroyed by the bomb. Left standing were the south wall, some nave arcading and the east end with its 1962 Hans Feibusch mural. Fortunately Pieter Coeke van Aelst's only painting in Britain had just been removed.

At the instigation of the Bishop of London, and £4.5m from the City and readers of *The Times*, the church was rebuilt with its now familiar frontage and reopened in 2002 as a Centre for Reconciliation and Peace. Prince Charles, who performed the opening ceremony, has welcomed the "sympathetic scheme for restoring a church which is one of the few survivors of medieval London". A new east window depicting St Ethelburga is by Helen Whittaker although the reordering has hidden the Feibusch mural.

The Centre's advisory council includes the Cardinal Archbishop of Westminster and the Chief Rabbi. The Director is former ambassador Roland Smith who sees relations between Islam and Christianity as a focus.

St Giles Cripplegate

This church in the Barbican has been likened to a ship in dry dock. St Giles is patron of cripples but Cripplegate probably comes from crepel meaning covered way. Cripplegate was a gateway with St Giles without, or outside, the City wall which survives here.

St Giles was founded sometime between 1080 and 1115. The present airy church is largely the building of about 1548 and has been described as "the last gasp of the medieval tradition". A fire at the end of Henry VIII's reign destroyed much of the 14th-century church but it was rebuilt to the same plan. The Great Fire missed Cripplegate but the Second World War bombing did not and the church was damaged. Restoration was completed in 1960 with a new cupola being added to the attractive tower which still has a 14th-century base. But the parish was much more badly damaged which led to the area being redeveloped as the Barbican. Wooden houses on the north side of the church gave way to the lake.

Oliver Cromwell was married here, John Bunyan and Daniel Defoe worshipped here and Holman Hunt, painter of *The Light of the World*, was baptised here. Buried in the church are John Foxe of *Book of Martyrs* fame and mariner Martin Frobisher. Poet John Milton's tomb was opened in 1793 by Verger Elizabeth Grant who charged 6d to anyone wanting to view it but was soon forced to reduce the fee to 2d.

William Shakespeare's nephew Edward was christened here in 1606 but lived only a year before being buried here. His actor father died the same year but is buried in Southwark's old priory church (Southwark Cathedral). There is by chance a monument to Margaret Lucy, granddaughter of Sir Thomas Lucy who is depicted as Justice Shallow in Shakespeare's *The Merry Wives of Windsor*.

Rectors include Lancelot Andrewes who, whilst here, helped with the Authorised Version of the Bible translation. This was the first City church to have a woman priest on the staff and Katharine Rumens is the City's first woman incumbent. She is also the first to have been a fashion designer with her own label.

Paul Middleton

St Helen's Bishopsgate

The rare dedication is to St Helen who in the 4th century searched the Holy Land for the places where Christ walked and by tradition is credited with discovering the True Cross.

The first mention of the church is in 1140. A Benedictine nunnery opened alongside in 1204 and this led in 1475 to the church having a double nave — one for the sisters and one for the parish. The wooden dividing screens were removed when the convent was dissolved in 1538.

There are so many memorials that this church has been called the City's Westminster Abbey. Some came in 1874 from the lost St Martin Outwich and include the effigies of Sir John de Oteswich and his wife in early Tudor dress. The great City figures buried here are Sir John Crosby, who paid for the double nave, and Sir Thomas Gresham who founded Gresham College in his own house nearby.

This is a remarkable example of a monastic building surviving both the Great Fire and the Second World War. However, it was badly shaken by IRA bombs in 1992 and again in 1993 when the Bishopsgate blast destroyed the nearby St Ethelburga's.

A controversial restoration and re-ordering by Quinlan Terry has left the church with a single floor level which reduces the impact of some monuments but allows for underfloor heating. A gallery has been added at the east end and the chancel screen moved to become the entrance to the south transept where the Holy Ghost and Lady Chapels were once found. Clear glass has replaced the shattered stained glass windows.

The focus of the church interior is the 1632 pulpit on the south side. This was its position when the parish nave had a chancel and screen but now the seats face not the east end but the south wall with the back rows being in the convent nave. This large capacity is needed on Tuesdays when lunchtime speakers draw a crowd large enough to have two performances.

An evangelical tradition means that the altar appears only for the Eucharist on the first Sunday of the month.

St James Garlickhythe

This church on Garlick Hill existed in at least 1170 when it was known as St James-apud-Viniteriam meaning near Vintry. Later it became St James-apud-Tamisyam meaning near the Thames. With garlic being regularly unloaded at the nearby hythe, the name then evolved into the familiar St James Garlickhythe.

Sometimes ships docked with pilgrims returning from the Galician coast having visited the shrine of the parish's patron St James the Great at Compostela. The church has numerous decorative shells, the symbol of St James who can be seen outside on top of the clock.

The old church was destroyed in the Great Fire so the present building is largely Wren's design with the tower added by Hawksmoor. The present church, known as Wren's Lantern, has the highest nave in the City with many 17th-century fittings from the now disappeared St Michael Queenhythe. The painting of the Ascension over the altar is by Andrew Geddes whose brother was a curate here in 1815.

In the First World War a bomb just missed the church and in thanksgiving an annual Bomb Sermon was preached for a decade. During the Second World War another bomb hit the church exposing the crypt but failed to explode. The device was raised 30 feet and taken to Hackney Marshes for detonation. However, in 1991 a 170 foot crane crashed through the roof between the very same pillars just missed by the bomb. Motorists on the road outside were saved from injury when the traffic lights changed to red seconds before the crane toppled from a building site opposite.

The Vintners' Company clutching posies to ward off smells walk here every summer led by a wine porter clearing the way with a broom. The Skinners come on Corpus Christi afternoon in a procession which has taken place annually in the City since 1393.

The church is home of the Prayer Book Society. Santiago pilgrims setting out on the long walk or cycle ride across France and Spain often call in to have their pilgrim 'credential' stamped.

Paul Middleton

St Katharine Cree

The first church was built about 1280 and called St Katharine de Christ Church at Aldgate as it stood in the grounds of a priory known as Christ Church. Cree is a corruption of Christ.

St Katharine's, although newly rebuilt, was pulled down when Henry VIII closed the priory. After a gap of exactly a century the present building was consecrated in 1631 by Archbishop Laud. The Leadenhall Street entrance to the church is through the base of the 1504 tower which survived. The top has a cupola added in 1776.

Katharine was tortured on a wheel which became her emblem and the focus here is the Catherine wheel window above the altar.

The reredcs below comes from the nearby St James Duke's Place which was demolished in 1874. Nearby is a monument to Sir Walter Raleigh's father-in-law Sir Nicholas Throkmorton who gave his name to Throgmorton Street. The organ dates from 1686 when it was tested by Purcell.

John Betjeman was unhappy about the offices built into the north and south aisles from which he could hear typing. These rooms, beyond the nave's Corinthian columns, make the church a centre of Christian activity. The City Churches Development Group (1998-2003), formed to increase public access to all City Churches, was based here and present occupiers include the Guild of All Souls, which issues a helpful leaflet about preparing for death, and the international Guild of Church Musicians. The offices date from 1963 when the church was the Industrial Christian Fellowship headquarters – hence the London Transport roundel at the back of the church.

Lloyd's Choir sings at major services such as the St James's Day evensong which is followed by a party in the enclosed churchyard. Lloyd's German Club holds a carol service at St Nicholas-tide. The font bears the arms of donor Lord Mayor Sir John Gayer who, in thanks for surviving an encounter with a lion whilst abroad in 1643, endowed the annual Lion Sermon. Preachers have included Terry Waite. On Sundays the Mar Thoma congregation worships here.

Paul Middleton

St Lawrence Jewry

The church, on the site since 1136, stands over a tiered section of the 7,000 seat Roman amphitheatre in use from AD 70 until the 4th century. The dedication is to a saint martyred by the Romans, as seen in the weathervane, and Jewry recalls that the parish was on the edge of the Jewish area.

The original building was destroyed by the Great Fire and Wren's replacement opened in 1677 in the presence of Charles II. His chaplain John Tillotson was the regular Tuesday Lecturer here before becoming Archbishop of Canterbury in 1691.

A century later it was the custom to print and circulate to the aldermen the Michaelmas Day sermon until "it was not found to be of any value in the direction and so was discontinued". With Guildhall nearby it was natural for the Corporation of London to use St Lawrence Jewry for its church services after the Guildhall Chapel became a court in 1782.

In 1940 the church was almost completely destroyed by a bomb. The rebuild is to a design by Cecil Brown who cleverly incorporated the vicarage into the building and made a spacious interior for civic occasions. The Queen followed the example of her predecessor by coming to the opening of the restored church in 1957.

The figure of St Thomas More in the window by the pulpit is a reminder that he preached here. The Commonwealth Chapel in the north side, with its national flags, marks the City of London's role in Commonwealth development.

The father of Gresham College founder Thomas Gresham, who gave his name to Gresham Street outside, is among the many buried here.

The organist is Catherine Ennis, formerly Assistant Organist at Christ Church Oxford and England's first woman cathedral organist, who gives lunchtime recitals. Sir Thomas Beecham's piano is used for piano recitals.

Annual events include the Plough Monday Service for Guildhall staff and the Candlemas service attended by the Tallow Chandlers' and Wax Chandlers' Companies.

Paul Middleton

St Magnus the Martyr

The first mention of the church is in 1067 when the newly arrived William I granted the patronage to Westminster Abbey. During Elizabeth I's reign the Rector was the Bible translator and former Bishop of Exeter Miles Coverdale.

In 1666 the church was one of the first to be consumed by the Great Fire which started at the top of the hill to the north.

Wren was responsible for the rebuild but this new church soon underwent some changes at the west end when the approach to London Bridge was widened in 1759. The paving under the tower portico was once the pavement running over the bridge. However, this commanding position at the entrance to the City was short-lived for in 1832 the new London Bridge was built some yards upstream.

A window on the south side depicts the St Thomas Becket Chapel on the bridge which paid an annual levy to St Magnus as compensation for loss of alms from visitors entering the City.

The clock was donated in 1709 by Lord Mayor Charles Duncombe who as a saddler's apprentice had been in trouble for arriving late from his home in Southwark. The windows on the church's north side were blocked as early as 1782 to reduce traffic noise from cobbled Lower Thames Street.

"Inexplicable splendour of Ionian white and gold" is TS Eliot's description in *The Waste Land*. Then the contrast with outside was heightened by the smell of Billingsgate fish market in the street giving way to incense inside.

Martin Travers rearranged the interior in the 1920s. The statue of St Magnus in a winged helmet dates from this time but the image is of the 12th-century St Magnus of Orkney. The church dedication is clearly to an earlier Magnus.

The catholic tradition was introduced in 1922 by Canon Henry Fiennes-Clinton who refounded the Fraternity of Our Lady de Salve Regina, originally a devotional guild for fishmongers. At his funeral in 1959 fish porters holding their traditional hats lined Lower Thames Street.

Paul Middleton

St Margaret Lothbury

Early names were St Margaret-upon-Lothberi and St Margaret de Lodeburi. The Walbrook stream flows below so Lothbury may refer to the lode or drain. In 1440 Lord Mayor Robert Large paid for the stream to be covered by a stone arch so that the church could be extended. At this time the church still belonged to Barking Abbey which suggests a Saxon foundation.

The church was destroyed by the Great Fire and rebuilt in 1690 by Wren using Portland stone. The tower, added in 1700, is probably the work of Hooke.

Many fittings have subsequently come from other churches. The impressive chancel screen is the same date as the church but was made for All Hallows Upper Thames Street which was demolished in 1894. John Betjeman noted that the screen "nearly knocks into the cherubs on the sounding board of the pulpit". All Hallows was a Wren church and St Margaret's is one of only two Wren churches in the City with a screen.

The 1801 George Pike England organ once played by Mendelssohn is just one of many items which came from St Olave Old Jewry after its demolition in 1879. The reredos is now flanked by paintings of Moses and Aaron from St Christopher-le-Stocks which was sold in 1782.

An important Rector was AJ Ingram whose brother W Rowlands Ingram in 1891 designed the screen separating the nave and south aisle. His son HC Ingram added the vestry and parish room in 1910.

With the back door of the Bank of England directly opposite this tiny church has become the Bankers' Church. Seminars held here have included a Living with Capitalism series. In December the Bankers' Carol Service has to be held twice to accommodate numbers.

Richard Townend, well-known for his lecture recitals and a pupil of Harold Darke and Herbert Howells, has given over 950 lunchtime organ recitals here in the course of more than thirty years as Resident Recitalist.

Paul middleton

St Margaret Pattens

The first record of the church is in 1067. Pattens probably refers to the iron and wood undershoes which raised the wearer's feet above the street mud. However there was a Ranulf Patin who owned land here and the church was called St Margaret de Patins. The church was rebuilt as late as 1538 and Rood Lane on the west side recalls this time when the cross was taken down from the rood screen and exhibited in the churchyard.

The present church is Wren's replacement following the Great Fire. The 199 foot spire was completed in 1701. Inside there are rare canopied churchwardens' pews. The pulpit has a holder for an hourglass, which can still be brought from the vestry to time a sermon, and the Lady Chapel has hooks for hanging wigs. Behind the high altar is 17th-century Carlo Maratti's painting *Christ in Gethsemane*.

In 1884 this was the first City church since the Reformation to use incense. The Rector, James Fish, introduced Choral Eucharists on important weekdays with Gounod and Haydn settings. He also managed to raise Sunday attendance from around three in the 1870s to over fifty by the time of his retirement in 1907.

The observance here of 30 January as Charles King and Martyr Day began with the incumbency of James Fish whose Rectory is now the Britannia building society. He added the Della Robbia tondo in the north aisle in memory of earlier Rector Thomas Wagstaffe who had been deprived of the living for loyalty to the exiled James II rather than William III. The Royal Arms at the west end are those of James II.

Rector for 21 years until 1984 was Gordon Huelin. As author of *Vanished Churches of the City of London* he knew much about the lost St Gabriel Fenchurch which amalgamated with the parish after the Great Fire. Alterations made to the church following war damage have enabled St Margaret's to provide offices for the Busoga Trust and space for a lunchtime keep fit class. As in the time of James Fish there is a weekday Choral Eucharist with the choir now provided by the Singers Workshop.

Paul Middleton

St Martin's Ludgate

This church, which existed in 1138, was once known as St Martin-the-Little and St Martin-the-Less to distinguish it from the now lost St Martin-le-Grand. The present correct name is St Martin-within-Ludgate which recalls that the church stood just inside the City's wall next to the Lud Gate.

The Great Fire destroyed the old church although the adjoining City gateway survived until being pulled down in 1760. The present building, unlike the first, is built hard against the City wall so that the west end is a Roman wall. Although parishioners gave Wren a hogshead of wine as a thankyou present it is widely believed that the church is mainly the work of Hooke who visited the site at least 31 times. It certainly has a Dutch feel which Hooke liked but Wren must have approved the Scandinavian spire which was to act as a foil to St Paul's dome.

The large entrance lobby, running the length of the south side and large enough to be used as a charity card shop in Advent, provides a useful double wall to insulate the main church from traffic noise.

The interior has an impressive 17th-century brass chandelier which was added in about 1740 having been brought mysteriously from St Vincent's Cathedral on St Vincent Island. Bread shelves from lost St Mary Magdalen Old Fish Street are filled with tempting bread but, sadly for today's hungry, the loaves are not real. Unique in the City is a double seat for the two churchwardens.

Rector Samuel Purchas was a friend of Princess Pocahontas who in 1616 stayed at the pub next door and so probably visited the old church. Admiral William Penn, as a young captain, came here for his wedding in 1634.

This is no longer a parish church and until recently the Priest-in-Charge was the Librarian of St Paul's. It was here that the daily services were held when the cathedral was closed during preparations for the Prince of Wales' wedding in 1981.

Until 2003 the Director of Music was Petronella Dittmer who maintained a very high standard of music. Annual services include the Old Bailey Carol Service.

Paul Middleton

St Mary Abchurch

The name of the church, first mentioned in 1198, is a shortened version of St Mary Abbechurch. But it was first called St Mary Upchurch because the patron was the Prior of Southwark who could see the church up the hill across the river from his priory – now Southwark Cathedral.

After the dissolution Archbishop Parker persuaded Elizabeth I to give it to his college Corpus Christi Cambridge which still appoints the incumbent.

The medieval building had side chapels and today a 14th-century crypt survives under the yard. But the church did not survive the Great Fire and rebuilding was completed in 1686 at the cost of £4,922 2s 5 1/2d.

Wren's brick church is square with a tower in the north-west corner. Simon Jenkins likens the approach to St Mary Abchurch to "the backwater of a Dutch provincial town". John Betjeman thought the interior to be "certainly one of the most beautiful in the City". The surprise is a shallow dome invisible from outside. This was another experiment which led to his great St Paul's masterpiece.

The focal point is the huge limewood reredos which is the only one in the City known for certain to have been designed by Grinling Gibbons. His bill for the "Olter Pees" was found as recently as 1946. The reredos was smashed into 2000 pieces by a wartime bomb and its reassembly took five years. In the centre is a pelican feeding her young which is the symbol of both the Eucharist celebrated below and also the crest of Corpus Christi College.

The font is by William Kempster, brother of Wren's stonemason Christopher. The pulpit is by another Wren craftsman William Gray. The Royal Arms are those of James II who had just come to the throne when the church opened. Some original pews survive but without their once popular dog kennels.

The flowers and fruit in the reredos and pulpit are appropriate for a church which has associations with the Fruiterers' Company whose arms appear in the south window. Restoration of the building was undertaken by Godfrey Allen between 1946 and 1958.

Paul Middleton

St Mary Aldermary

The earliest mention of a church here is 1080 and it was almost certainly of Saxon origin. St Mary de Eldermariechurche became St Mary Aldermary with Aldermary derived from older Mary meaning older than nearby St Mary-le-Bow.

Numerous Lord Mayors and Shakespeare's fellow actors Heming and Condell were buried in the pre-Fire church. Rector Henry Gold was sentenced by the Star Chamber to 'stand in Paul's all the sermon time' before being executed at Tyburn. John Milton married his third wife here in 1662.

The address is Watling Street although the front door is in Bow Lane which John Betjeman called "the last surviving City alley of shops". On the south side is Ye Olde Watling which was the works canteen for stonemasons rebuilding St Paul's.

This has been described as the most important late 17th-century gothic church in the country due to the fan vault ceiling which is comparable to the one to be found in Westminster Abbey's Henry VII Chapel. This is the only parish church to have such a ceiling.

St Mary's was rebuilt under the direction of Wren and it is not only the more mysterious of his churches but his only gothic-style church. It may reflect the earlier building which had only been completed in Henry VIII's reign. The parishioners are thought to have wanted a restoration rather than allow Wren a free hand and certainly fire damaged stone was used.

The tower escaped damage in the Great Fire but succumbed to the 1703 Great Storm. The church's south side was obscured from view until the building of Queen Victoria Street in the 1860s suddenly exposed it. This resulted in a refacing in stone in the 1870s.

The organist is Claire Conley Hill who plays on an instrument dating from 1781 and can often be heard in the afternoons. The church no longer has any livery links although the arms of the Innholders', Vintners' and Salters' Companies appear in the windows. John Mothersole was licensed recently as Priest-in-Charge after a long interregnum.

St Mary-le-Bow

The church dates from 1087. Bow is a reference to arches in the vaulted crypt where the Court of Arches, the ecclesiastical court, sits.

The claim that to be a cockney you must be born within the sound of Bow Bells really means between St Mary-le-Bow and Bow Church in East London. The Great Bell of Bow, which called Dick Whittington back to London, is in the 224 foot tower which Wren provided for the rebuild after the Great Fire. The BBC broadcast the 12 bell peal during the Second World War as a call sign for people listening secretly abroad.

The present church is the result of a redesign by Laurence King following Second World War bombing which left mainly the crypt and the steeple intact. Inside, the suspended rood cross, carved in Oberammergau, is by John Hayward who is also responsible for the windows. His Sherborne Abbey window design was the subject of a Court of Arches hearing downstairs.

In 1983 the Rector said: "I would not like it to be thought that the prime concern is to hold services." Today's weekday ministry is the result of the outstanding incumbency of his successor Victor Stock, now Dean of Guildford. The unusual twin pulpits are used for the lunchtime dialogues which began under Joseph McCulloch and resumed under Victor Stock. Jeffrey Archer, Trevor McDonald and Diana Rigg have all been put on the spot. In the crypt is the award-winning Place Below vegetarian café open for breakfast and lunch.

Today visitors come from Trinity, Wall Street which was founded in 1697 when the Bishop of London's charter for the New York mission stated: "All shall there be ordered as it is in the Church of St Mary-le-Bow". A September 11 book of condolence signed here was taken by hand to Trinity as its congregation recovered from being trapped by the cloud of dust.

This is also London's Australian Church with a special service on Australia Day when Admiral Arthur Philip's baptism here is recalled. On Sundays, when Anglican commuters are at home, the church is filled by the St Thomas Syrian Orthodox Church.

St Mary-at-Hill

This church has been on the hillside since at least 1177 when it was attached to the Abbot of Waltham's house. This stood on the site of the Rectory which straddles an alley.

Much of the church, rebuilt early in Henry VIII's reign, survived the Great Fire so this was one of the first to be restored by Christopher Wren.

In 1894, when it just avoided demolition for the Underground, 3000 bodies were removed from the crypt and taken to Norwood Cemetery. This was the time when the Fellowship Porters, who had an annual service here on the Sunday after St John the Baptist's Day, was dissolved by the Corporation of London. The mention of the fictional Six Jolly Fellowship Porters pub in *Our Mutual Friend* suggests that Charles Dickens was familiar with the area.

The Lovat Lane approach from Eastcheap is still narrow but the smell of fish from Billingsgate Market down the hill, mixed with coffee from the grinder in Botolph Alley, has cleared.

John Betjeman described the church as "the least spoiled and most gorgeous interior in the City". Sadly the box pews were lost during a 10-hour fire in 1988 but this was not as disastrous as it at first appears on entering the church because some fittings are in storage. For now the building seems larger and has a new beauty with its moveable chairs and a simple altar below a huge curtain where there was once a reredos.

This is the Fish Church since this is where the Fish Harvest Festival is held in October. The tradition of laying out a large slab with 39 varieties of fish resembling a fishmonger's, once complete with seaweed rushed at dawn from Brighton, has survived Billingsgate's move to Docklands. The only Sunday services are the autumn harvest festivals when there is also the Bakers' Thanksgiving complete with a display of different loaves in front of the altar.

The fish is distributed afterwards to Church Army homes in a tradition which began when CA founder William Carlile was rector from 1892 until 1926. Today's incumbent, Archdeacon Brian Kirk-Duncan, was appointed in 1962.

Paul Middleton

St Mary Moorfields

This is the City's only Roman Catholic church and takes its name from Moorfields, the moor on which the first church was erected in 1817. The entrance was on Bloomfield Street, with the altar unusually at the west end, and the south wall alongside the short eastern entrance to Finsbury Circus. An indication of the imposing facade can be found at St John the Baptist in Brighton where the entrance is modelled on this church.

This first St Mary Moorfields, which in 1850 became the temporary cathedral containing Cardinal Wiseman's throne, was demolished in 1899 and the site sold to help pay for Westminster Cathedral. The architect of the present smaller church, opened in 1903 in nearby Eldon Street, was George Sherrin who had been responsible for Brompton Oratory's dome.

The modest Portland stone entrance is slotted between shops with a narrow passage running under the presbytery. The church is lit by high small windows and the liturgical east end is on the north side to allow a direct view of the sanctuary from the doorway.

The immediate impression is of a grand bathroom. The altar was intended as Wiseman's sarcophagus. It is flanked by six 18 foot high marble columns from the old church and has a large blue marble backdrop. The first church had a dramatic panorama of the crucifixion featuring fifty larger than life figures by Italian scene-painter Agostino Aglio. The new church was provided with a copy which remained in position behind the altar until 1964 when it was removed for renovation. Unfortunately the rolled up canvas was never returned having been allegedly delivered by mistake to St Patrick's Soho.

There is one Mass on Sunday but on weekdays there are two. On special weekdays such as Ash Wednesday or Ascension Day the church is uncomfortably packed to standing room. After the lunchtime Mass on the last Friday in the month, here in the richest part of London, there are prayers for the poor.

This has been a City church only since 1994 when the City boundary was moved from the front to the back of the church.

St Mary Woolnoth

The site was a Roman temple and the earliest mention of a church is in 1191. At first it was known as St Mary of the Nativity but either the name of the founder, Wulfnoth, or the proximity of a wool market led to Wolnoth and now Woolnoth. A newspaper once called it St Mary Woolworth.

Much of the church survived the Great Fire but parishioners thought it unsafe and in 1716 the entire building was pulled down.

This is Hawksmoor's smallest church and his only City church. The frontage is similar to his colleague Vanbrugh's Seaton Delaval mansion in Northumberland built at the same time. The north side in Lombard Street has been compared with "the best of Continental Baroque architecture". The south side was little seen until King William Street opened in 1838.

A bronze of the Virgin Mary extends her arms in welcome above the entrance. The interior is a square based on the Egyptian Hall described by Vitruvius which was also to be the inspiration for the Mansion House banqueting hall. The east end is dominated by a baldacchino with barley-sugar columns inspired by drawings of the Temple at Jerusalem which fascinated Hawksmoor. The high Corinthian columns in the corners take the eye up to the arms of Elizabeth II added in 1968. Memorials include Lloyd's founder Edward Lloyd who died in 1712.

The pulpit was used by John Newton, author of the hymn *Amazing Grace*, who was Rector for 28 years from 1779. His preaching inspired William Wilberforce to battle against slavery. The church was nearly demolished in the 1890s to make way for the underground railway but instead Bank Underground Station's booking office opened in the crypt. The north-west doorway with cherubs heads was a station entrance.

The last Rector Richard Hayes sought to restore the interior to the original Hawksmoor magnificence and boosted funds by being sponsored by parish bankers to undertake the Scottish Coast to Coast walk. One morning he celebrated the Eucharist in walking boots before going downstairs to the Underground with a backpack.

Paul Middleton.

St Michael's Cornhill

The first church was Saxon. The Abbot of Evesham was patron from 1055 to 1503 when the Drapers' Company took over.

Rebuilding the church after the Great Fire began within just three years so Wren had little or no influence on the design. The 1420s tower survived and in 1722 was remodelled by Hawksmoor to resemble Magdalen's tower in Oxford.

The City's first coffee house began in a tent in the churchyard in 1657. Most financial business was done in coffee houses and nearby Lloyd's can trace its origin to a coffee house. Thomas Gray of Gray's Elegy fame was baptised here in 1716.

The building is now the City's most Victorian church following a refitting by Sir George Gilbert Scott in the late 1850s. The carved pews with their doors date from this time as does the round east window depicting Christ in Glory. Below is the reredos incorporating two 17th-century paintings of Aaron and Moses. The dramatic wooden carving of a pelican at the west end is 18th-century. Scott is also responsible for the impressive street entrance with St Michael over the doorway.

The incumbent is also Chaplain to the Stock Exchange which provides refreshments for the carol service sponsored by the *Mail on Sunday*. Another major event is the City's New Year service held early in January in the presence of the Lord Mayor.

St Michael's is known for its high standard of music. There has been an organ here since 1459 and once a resident choir lived in the cloister. Directors of Music include William Boyce, George II's Master of the King's Music; Richard Limpus, founder the Royal College of Organists (now at St Andrew's Holborn) and Richard Popplewell who became Organist, Choirmaster and Composer to Her Majesty's Chapels Royal. It was here in 1916 that composer Harold Darke started the City Church tradition of lunchtime recitals. By the time he retired in 1966 he had given over 1,800 organ performances. His successor Jonathan Rennert has now given over 340 Monday lunchtime recitals.

Paul Middleton

St Michael Paternoster Royal

In 1219 the church was called St Michael Paternosterchierrch but by 1361 it had become St Michael in the Riole. Now both words are used making Paternoster Royal today's name. Paternoster (Our Father) recalls the rosary makers working nearby and Royal is derived from La Réole in France from where Bordeaux wine was shipped to a nearby wharf.

The church was rebuilt in 1409 thanks to rich neighbour Dick Whittington who is buried here. After the Great Fire the church was one of the last to receive Wren's attention and the tower was not completed until 1713. William Butterfield, who had just seen his St Alban's Holborn masterpiece completed, rearranged the interior in 1866. However, all this was lost in 1944 when a German flying bomb came through the roof leaving only Wren's walls and tower.

The bombing also opened the south side of this previously hidden church to the main road. Today's restored church was completed in 1968 and opened by Prince Philip. The former side entrance has become the main doorway whilst the old entrance in College Hill now leads to Whittington Hall. The 1644 candelabra came in 1893 from the now demolished All Hallows the Great. The new windows are by John Hayward. The main east end window depicts St Michael. The Whittington window shows Dick Whittington, his cat and the streets paved with gold.

After the Great Fire the Whittington tomb remained unmarked but recently an inscription in gold lettering – Richard Whittington mercer 1358-1423 – has been cut in the stone floor: after the War a cat was found buried here but the one in the Whittington story may refer to a boat.

This is appropriate for the church is now the headquarters of The Mission to Seafarers, formerly the Missions to Seamen. The church has a fine banner featuring not only the new name but the new flying angel logo. From here the Mission provides back-up for over 300 chaplains in ports around world who offer friendship as well as practical and spiritual help to seafarers. The Princess Royal, the society's president, is a regular visitor to the church.

Paul Middleton

St Nicholas Cole Abbey

The church is first mentioned in 1144 and was once known as St Nicholas-behind-Fish Street. Old Fish Street Hill runs along the east end and in Elizabethan times there was a fish tank fed by the Thames attached to the outside north wall.

A later name was Cold Abbey derived from cold harbour meaning shelter for travellers.

Being dedicated to St Nicholas, the church kept the tradition of electing a boy bishop on St Nicholas Day up to the Reformation. After Mary's accession, which followed Edward VI's Protestant reign, this was the first church in London to celebrate the Mass in Latin with a cross and candles on the altar. A century later the patronage belonged to Puritan Colonel Hacker, guard commander at Charles I's execution.

After the Great Fire this was the first London church rebuilt by Wren. The churchwardens resisted Charles II's wish to give the site to the Lutherans. (They eventually moved into another City Church on the 300th anniversary of the Great Fire.) The bill for the work in 1678 included 6d for "half a pint of canary for Dr Wren's coachmen".

The front door was on the north side but when Queen Victoria Street was built across the churchyard in 1871 the back door became the main entrance with a gilded statue of St Nicholas above a gateway. After this time it was known as St Nicholas Coal Hole due to the blackened interior caused by smoke seeping up from the underground trains below.

Rector from 1883 to 1900 was the leading Christian Socialist Henry Shuttleworth who made the church a centre for debate complete with a bar. He is said to be the model for the jolly cleric Morell in Bernard Shaw's *Candida*.

Fire bombs gutted the church in 1941 and its grim state can be seen in the 1951 film *The Lavender Hill Mob* where a bullion robbery is staged outside. By 1962 the building was restored with a new taller spire and dramatic stained glass by Keith New. The Free Church of Scotland occupied the church between 1982 and 2003.

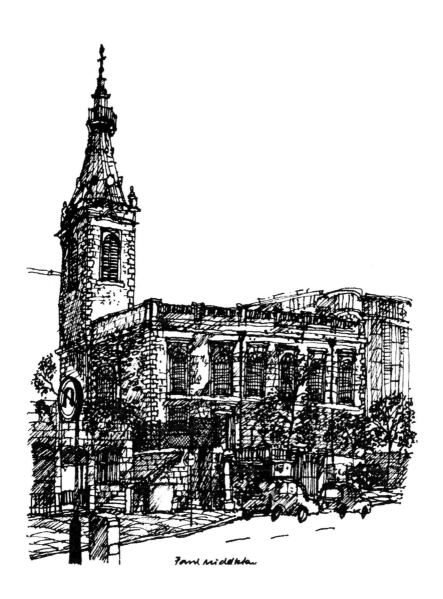

Paul Middleton

St Olave's Hart Street

The church was probably founded by the Saxons since the dedication is to King Olaf of Norway who in 1014 helped Londoners turn back invading Danes on the Thames. It was known as St Olave-towards-the-Tower in 1222 but by 1405 it had become St Olave-in-Hertstrete.

The 13th-century crypt survives and the above ground building is largely 15th-century thanks to Admiral William Penn and Admiralty Secretary Samuel Pepys who had houses blown up to stop the Great Fire reaching here. The Navy Office was in Seething Lane and the church had an outside staircase leading to the Navy pew. Pepys and his wife Elizabeth are buried by the high altar. Her memorial (erected by him) is in the sanctuary and his memorial is on the south wall marking the position of the Navy door.

Bombs hit the church in 1941 but important contents had been moved to St Paul's Cathedral crypt. King Haakon VII of Norway laid the new foundation stone in 1951 so the sanctuary entrance is now flanked by a stone mitre and the Norwegian Crown. The post-war Rectory in Hart Street has a carving of St Olaf by Norwegian Carl Schou.

The description in Dickens' *Uncommercial Traveller* of the Seething Lane entrance remains accurate: "…a small small churchyard, with a ferocious strong spiked iron gate, like a jail. This gate is ornamented with skulls and cross bones, larger than life wrought in stone." Burials include Mary Ramsey who is reputed to have brought the Great Plague to London. Betjeman likened St Olave's to a country church.

Annual events here include the Pepys Commemoration Service addressed by a noted Pepys expert, the Trinity House Service attended by its Master Prince Philip and the Wine and Spirit Trade's Vintage Harvest Festival when decorations include hops. This is also the church of the Clothworkers' Company who hold a Christmas carol service on the Eve of St Thomas's Day, a traditional day for almsgiving always observed by the Clothworkers. A Millennium window shows St Thomas holding a bag of money.

Paul Middleton

St Peter's Cornhill

It is claimed that the first church here opened in AD 179. However, it appears to have closed by the time St Augustine arrived in 596 and the next mention is 1040. The Whit Monday procession to St Paul's always started at St Peter's, being considered the oldest City church, and in 1979 there were celebrations marking the 18th centenary year.

St Peter upon Cornhill was in the corn market on the City's highest ground, a hill. The medieval church was badly damaged by the Great Fire and the present brick building by Wren opened in 1682 with the tower completed two years later. The frontage in Gracechurch Street is set back ten feet from the old foundation to allow a widening of the street. But the 140 foot steeple, with a St Peter's key weathervane, rests on a pre-Fire tower base.

The best view is from the recently landscaped churchyard in St Peter's Alley. Charles Dickens, in *Our Mutual Friend*, describes its appearance in the 19th century as "a churchyard; a paved court, with a raised bank of earth about breast high, in the middle, enclosed by iron rails". Now its a summer overspill for drinkers from the Counting House.

Inside is the only City church chancel screen by Wren to be in its original position. The Rector, the future Bishop of St Asaph William Beveridge, insisted on having a screen although Wren was against it. The compromise was one which emphasises the sanctity of the chancel but is delicate enough to allow an almost clear view of the altar. The reredos is a low structure with light flooding into the otherwise dark church from the windows above.

The pillars dividing the nave from the aisles probably follow the medieval pattern for Wren used the old foundations.

Mendelssohn twice came here to play the 1861 Father Smith organ which he declared to be "the finest in London".

Although a notice declares this to be 'the church of the British Sailors Society' this has long ceased to be so. The incumbent was its honorary chaplain but now the building is used as a study centre by St Helen's.

Paul Middleton

St Sepulchre's

This, the City's largest church, was called St Edmund's when first mentioned in 1137 but soon became the Church of the Holy Sepulchre or St Sepulchre-without-Newgate. It is, like Jerusalem's Holy Sepulchre, just outside the old north-west gate of the city.

The church's tower survives from the 15th century but the nave was rebuilt after the Great Fire. Rector John Rogers, who helped William Tyndale to translate the Bible, became the Reformation's first Protestant martyr when burnt to death in Smithfield. The church ministered to many Roman Catholic martyrs on their way from nearby Newgate Prison (now the Old Bailey) to the Tyburn gallows. Both Shakespeare and Dickens refer to the bell sounding for those who had been condemned. This is either the church's 'Bells of Old Bailey' or the bell on show which was rung outside the cells.

Next door is the Watch House dating from 1791 and intended as the churchyard's guardhouse to deter body snatchers employed by nearby St Bartholomew's Hospital. On the tiny building is the bust of Charles Lamb who knew the church when he was a pupil at Christ's Hospital which stood opposite. Until recently the school used to return once a year by train from its new Sussex home for an annual service. By tradition the pupils laid bets during the journey on the length of the sermon.

This is the Musicians' Church where Peter Mullen, author of *A History of Promenade Concerts*, is the incumbent. The wreath placed on Sir Henry Wood's bust during the Last Night of the Proms is brought here the next day to be with his ashes in the church where he was Assistant Organist at the age of 14.

A large window depicts Captain John Smith who was saved from death by Princess Pocahontas and is buried here. He is seen holding a map of Virginia where he was the first Governor. Author Patricia Cornwell visited the church whilst researching her book *Isle of Dogs* but her plan to donate seven large stained glass windows honouring the Virginia link has run into difficulties. Wren designed the church to have clear glass to let in "God's light".

St Stephen Walbrook

The Lord Mayor's parish church behind the Mansion House used to be known as St Stephen-super-Walbrook after the now hidden stream which flows along the west side.

Today's Wren building is one of his largest churches and quite unlike any other in the City. It is also Britain's earliest domed church and an experiment for St Paul's Cathedral. Italian sculptor Canova expressed a wish to visit England just to see St Paul's, Somerset House and St Stephen Walbrook. Within twenty years of completion – the tower is probably by Hawksmoor – the church was said to be "famous all over Europe and justly reputed... perhaps Italy itself can produce no modern buildings that can vie with this in taste or proportion".

Palladio called the church "the finest proportioned enclosed building in the world".

The driving force for the ambitious rebuild after the Great Fire was the churchwardens. In the 20th-century former churchwarden Lord Palumbo was been responsible for both saving the church from the seeping waters of the Walbrook and for a controversial interior reordering. This dispenses with traditional pews to make a Henry Moore altar the focus below the dome. Critics likened this to a "ripe camembert cheese" and the design led to a rare sitting of the Court of Ecclesiastical Causes Reserved. As the controversy raged the carved travertine marble altar stood in a field with sheep near Moore's studio at Much Hadham.

Today the carefully restored church has a light and spacious feel which appealed to Princess Margaret's daughter Lady Sarah Armstrong-Jones who chose to be married here.

Funerals include Marcus Morris, founder of *Eagle* comic, who died in 1989. One of his contributors was Chad Varah who was appointed Rector in 1953 and has become even more famous than his church. Here he founded the Samaritans using a telephone still to be seen at the back of the church.

The Lord Mayor and the household are away at weekends so the Sunday Sung Eucharist is now on Thursday.

Paul Middleton

St Vedast

Vedast was Bishop of Arras and is well known in Belgium although in England the dedication is only found here and at Tathwell in Lincolnshire. This City church dates from at least 1249.

The church, behind the new coffee bar on the corner of Cheapside, is often known as St Vedast-alias-Foster but as the sole survivor of an amalgamation of 13 parishes it can claim to have the longest name of any City church – St Vedast with St Michael-le-Querne, St Matthew Friday Street, St Peter Cheap, St Alban Wood Street, St Olave Silver Street, St Michael Wood Street & St Mary Staining, St Anne & St Agnes and St John Zachary Gresham Street.

The south wall still includes medieval material from the first church where poet Robert Herrick was baptised in 1591. The rebuild after the Great Fire was completed in 1699 but the architect was probably Hooke rather than Wren. 150 years later the church became well-known for Gregorian chant.

Today's collegiate-style interior is a result of restoration by Stephen Dykes Bower after severe Second World War damage. It is appropriate that some furnishings come from lost City churches including one in the present parish. The Royal Arms came from St Matthew Friday Street. The reredos was once in St Christopher-le-Stocks and the pulpit at All Hallows Bread Street.

A surprise for visitors is the delightful hidden cloister linking the church to the rectory and the hall built in 1691. Until the bombing it was possible to pick blackberries here.

Incumbents include Archbishop Rotherham, Edward IV's Lord Chancellor; Gonville ffrench-Beytagh who came as the deported Dean of Johannesburg and the present Bishop of Kensington Michael Colclough who celebrated his first Mass as a bishop here.

Today's Director of Music is versatile Joanna Paul who regularly brings her acclaimed Bayswater Blasters children's choir to sing from the gallery on Sundays.

This, the church of the Pewterers, Goldsmiths and Saddlers, is a quiet holy space in the City.

Paul Middleton

Church Addresses

All Hallows-by-the-Tower
Byward Street 020 7481 2928
www.allhallowsbythetower.org.uk
Underground: Tower Hill
Open: Monday to Friday 9am-6pm &
weekends 10am-5pm

All Hallows-on-the-Wall
London Wall 020 7588 8064
www.onthewall.org
Underground: Liverpool Street
Open: Last Friday of month 12.30pm-
2pm

St Andrew's Holborn
Holborn Circus 020 7353 3544
www.standrewholborn.org.uk
Underground: Chancery Lane or
Farringdon
Open: Monday to Friday 8am-5.30pm
(Wednesday 2pm)

St Andrew Undershaft
St Mary Axe 020 7283 2231
Underground: Aldgate
Not open to the public

St Andrew-by-the-Wardrobe
www.standrew.freewire.co.uk
Queen Victoria Street 020 7248 7546
Underground: Blackfriars
Open: Monday to Friday 10am-4pm

St Anne & St Agnes
Gresham Street 020 7606 4986
www.stanneslutheranchurch.org
Underground: St Paul's
Open: 9am-6pm

The Dutch Church Austin Friars
Austin Friars 020 7588 1684
www.dutchchurch.org.uk
Underground: Bank
Open: Tuesday to Friday 11am-3pm

St Bartholomew the Great
Smithfield 020 7606 5171
www.greatstbarts.com
Underground: St Paul's
Open: Sunday 8am-1pm & 2.30pm-
8pm; Tuesday to Friday 8.30am-5pm;
Saturday 10.30am-1.30pm

St Bartholomew the Less
Smithfield 020 7601 8066
Underground: St Paul's
Open: 7am-8pm

St Benet's Welsh Church
Queen Victoria Street 020 7489 8754
Underground: Blackfriars
Open: Sunday services 11am &
2.30pm

St Botolph's Aldersgate
Aldersgate Street 020 7606 0684
Underground: St Paul's
Open: Monday to Friday 11am-3pm
(Thursday 12.45-2.30pm)

St Botolph's Aldgate
Aldgate 020 7283 1670
Underground: Aldgate
Open: Monday to Friday 10am-3pm

St Botolph's Bishopsgate
Bishopsgate 020 7588 3388
www.stbotolphs.org.uk
Underground: Liverpool Street
Open: Monday to Friday 8am-5.30pm

St Bride's Fleet Street
Fleet Street 020 7427 0133
www.stbrides.com
Underground: Blackfriars
Open: Monday to Saturday 8am-5pm

St Clement's Eastcheap
Clement's Lane 020 7626 4481
Underground: Monument
Open: Monday to Friday 7am-5pm

St Dunstan-in-the-West
Fleet Street 020 7405 1929
Underground: Temple
Open: Sunday 8am-3pm; Monday
9am-2pm; Tuesday 11am-3pm;
Wednesday 12.30-2.30pm; Friday
4.30-7.30pm; Saturday 1-7pm

St Edmund the King
Lombard Street 020 7626 9701
Underground: Bank
Reopens late 2003

St Ethelburga's
Centre for Reconciliation & Peace
78 Bishopsgate 020 7496 1610
www.stethelburgas.org
Underground: Liverpool Street
Open: Wednesday 11am-3pm

St Giles Cripplegate
Barbican 020 7638 1997
www.stgilescripplegate.com
Underground: Barbican or Moorgate
Open: Monday to Friday 11am-4pm

St Helen's Bishopsgate
Great St Helen's, off Bishopsgate 020
7283 2231
www.st-helens.org.uk
Underground: Liverpool Street
Open: Monday to Friday 9am-5pm

St James Garlickhythe
Garlick Hill 020 7236 1719
www.stjamesgarlickhythe.org.uk
Underground: Mansion House
Open: Monday to Friday 10am-4pm

St Katharine Cree
Leadenhall Street 020 7283 5733
Underground: Aldgate East
Open: Monday to Friday 10.30am-
4pm

St Lawrence Jewry
Gresham Street 020 7600 9478
Underground: Bank
Open: Monday to Friday 7.30am-2pm

St Magnus the Martyr
Lower Thames Street 020 7626 4481
Underground: Monument
Open: Tuesday to Friday 10am-4pm

St Margaret Lothbury
Lothbury 020 7606 8330
www.stml.org.uk
Underground: Bank
Open: Monday to Friday 7am-7pm

St Margaret Pattens
Eastcheap 020 7623 6630
Underground: Monument
Open: Monday to Friday 10am-4pm

St Martin's Ludgate
Ludgate Hill 020 7248 6054
Underground: Blackfriars
Open: Monday to Friday 11am-4pm

St Mary Abchurch
Abchurch Yard 020 7626 0306
Underground: Bank
Open: Wednesday 12 noon to 2pm

St Mary Aldermary
Bow Lane 020 7248 4906
www.stmaryaldermary.co.uk
Underground: Mansion House
Open: Monday to Friday 11am-3pm

St Mary-le-Bow
Cheapside 020 7248 5139
www.stmarylebow.co.uk
Underground: Bank
Open: Monday to Thursday 7.30am-
6pm; Friday 7.30am-4pm

St Mary-at-Hill
Lovat Lane 020 7626 4184
Underground: Monument
Open: Monday to Friday 11am-4pm

St Mary Moorfields
Eldon Street 020 7247 8390
www.stmarymoorfields.net
Underground: Liverpool Street
Open: Monday to Friday 7am-6.30pm

St Mary Woolnoth
Lombard Street 020 7626 9701
Underground: Bank
Open: Monday to Friday 9.30am-
4.30pm

St Michael's Cornhill
Cornhill 020 7248 3826
www.st-michaels.org.uk
Underground: Bank
Open Monday to Friday 8.30am-5pm

St Michael Paternoster Royal
College Street 020 7248 5202
Underground: Mansion House
Open: Monday to Friday 9am-5pm

St Nicholas Cole Abbey
Queen Victoria Street
Not open to the public

St Olave's, Hart Street
Hart Street 020 7488 4318
Underground: Tower Hill
Open: Monday to Friday 9am-5pm

St Peter's Cornhill
Cornhill 020 7283 2231
Underground: Bank
Not open to the public

St Sepulchre's
Holborn Viaduct 020 7248 3826
www.st-michaels.org.uk/sepulchre
Underground: St Paul's
Open: Tuesday to Thursday 12 noon
-2pm

St Stephen Walbrook
Walbrook 020 7283 4444
Underground: Bank
Open: Monday to Thursday 10am-
4pm; Friday 10am-3pm

St Vedast
Foster Lane 020 7606 3998
www.vedast.net
Underground: St Paul's
Open: Monday to Friday 8am-6pm

Other Addresses

City Deanery Office
St Botolph-without-Bishopsgate
Bishopsgate EC2M 3TL
020 7588 3388

The Friends of the City Churches
St Magnus the Martyr
Lower Thames Street EC3R 6DN
020 7626 1555
www.london-city-churches.org.uk

City Events
A monthly publication listing events in
City Churches.
St Vedast
4 Foster Lane EC2V 6HH
020 7606 3998
www.cityevents.co.uk

Select Bibliography

Betjeman, John *The City of London Churches* (Pitkin 1974)

Biddle, Martin *The Tomb of Christ* (Sutton 1999)

Blatch, Mervyn *A Guide to London Churches* (Constable 1978)

Bradley, Simon & Pevsner, Nikolaus *London: The City Churches*
(Penguin 1994)

Bryant, Chris *Possible Dreams: A personal history of the British
Christian Socialists* (Hodder 1996)

Du Prey, Pierre de la Ruffinière *Hawksmoor's London Churches*
(University of Chicago Press 2000)

Huelin, Gordon *Vanished Churches of the City of London* (Guildhall
Library 1996)

Humphrey, Stephen & Morris, James *Churches and Cathedrals of
London* (New Holland 2000)

Hyde, Ralph *Panoramania!* (Trefoil 1988)

Jeffery, Paul *The City of London Churches of Sir Christopher Wren*
(Hambledon 1996)

Jenkins, Simon *England's Thousand Best Churches* (Pengiun 2000)

Kendall, Derek *The City of London Churches: A Pictorial Rediscovery*
(Collins & Brown 1998)

Leech, Kenneth *Through Our Long Exile* (DLT 2001)

Stock, Victor *Taking Stock: Confessions of a City Priest*
(HarperCollins 2001)

Tinniswood, Adrian *His Invention So Fertile: a Life of Christopher
Wren* (Cape 2001)

Turner, Christopher *London Churches Step by Step* (Faber 1987)

Weinreb, Ben & Hibbert, Christopher *The London Encyclopaedia*
(Macmillan 1993)

Yates, Nigel *Anglican Ritualism in Victorian Britain 1830-1910*
(Oxford 1999)

Index

Adams, John Quincy 10
Addington, Henry 14
Addison, Joseph 42
Aelst, Pieter Coeke van 44
Aglio, Agostino 72
All Hallows Bread Street 90
All Hallows Upper Thames Street 58
All Hallows the Great 78
All Saints Pavement York 38
Allen, Godfrey 64
Allen, Sir William 32
Alleyn, Edward 32
Amos Trust 12
Appleton, Bishop George 30
Andrewes, Bishop Lancelot 10, 46
Archer, Lord 68
Armstrong-Jones, Sarah 88
Ayrton, Michael 28

Bakers' Thanksgiving 70
Bailey, Arthur 40
Baltic Exchange 16
Baltimore USA 38
Bangalore 9
Barking Abbey 10, 44, 58
Barnet, Battle of 40
Batty, Bishop Basil 20
Beecham, Sir Thomas 54
Bentham, Jeremy 30
Bentley, John Francis 30, 32,
Betjeman, Sir John 30, 42, 44, 52, 58, 64, 66, 70, 82
Beveridge, Bishop William 84
Billingsgate Market 70
Binney, Marcus 6
Bodley, Thomas 16, 24
Bomb Sermon 50
Boyce, William 76
Bow Church 68
Bray, Thomas 30
Brighton 70, 72
British Sailors Society 84
Brown, Arthur 22
Brown, Cecil 54

Brown, George 18
Brunel, Isambard Kingdom 14
Brunel, Marc 14
Bubble Sermon 34
Bulmer-Thomas, Ivor 18
Bulstrode Park House 18
Bunyan, John 46
Butchart, W 36
Butchers' Company 22
Butterfield, William 36, 78

Canova, Antonio 88
Carew, Sir Nicholas 30
Carlile, William 70
Charles I 20, 38
Charles II 42, 80
Charles, Prince of Wales 44
Chartres, Bishop Richard 6, 7, 34
Chatterton, Thomas 14
Christ Church Newgate 28
Christ Church Oxford 54
Christ's Hospital 86
Christian Aid 7, 12
Christian-Jewish Understanding,
Council for 30
Church Army 70
Church Musicians, Guild of 52
City Events 9
City Churches Development Group 7
City Corporation 7, 70
Clayton, Tubby 10
Clewer Sisters 18
Clothworkers' Company 82
Coke, Sir Edward 14
Colclough, Bishop Michael 90
Coles, Michael 10
College of Arms 26
Cologne 6
Comper, Sir Ninian 36
Condell, Henry 66
Conley Hill, Claire 66
Coram, Thomas 14
Cornwell, Patricia 86
Corpus Christi College Cambridge 64
Cortona, Pietro da 12
Court of Arches 68

Coverdale, Bishop Miles 40, 56
Creffield, Dennis 8
Cromwell, Oliver 46
Crosby, Sir John 48
Customs & Excise 10
Cyprus & the Gulf Diocese 10

Daily Courant 34
Daily Express 34
Daily Mail 34, 38
Dance, George the Elder 30, 32
Dance, George the Younger 12, 24
Dance-Holland, Nathaniel 12
Darcy, Lord 30
Darke, Harold 58, 76
de Bohun, Humphry 40
de Worde, Wynkyn 12, 34
Defoe, Daniel 30, 46
Dempster, Nigel 34
Dickens, Charles 70, 82, 84, 86
Disraeli, Benjamin 14
Dittmer, Petronella 62
Drapers' Company 76
Dryden, John 34, 44
Dulwich College 32
Dykes Bower, Stephen 90
Donne, John 38

Eagle 88
Earle, Bishop Alfred 32
Eastbourne 22
Easton, Hugh 24
Edward IV 90
Edward VI 16, 40
Eliot, TS 56
Elizabeth I 38
Elizabeth, Queen Mother 30
Ellison, Bishop Gerald 32
English Heritage 7
Ennis, Catherine 54
Erasmus, Desiderius 40
Etty, William 42
Evelyn, John 34
Evening News 34
Evesham, Abbot of 76

Feibusch, Hans 44
ffrench-Beytagh, Gonville 90
Fiennes-Clinton, Henry 56
Fielding, Henry 26
Fish Harvest Festival 70
Fish, James 60
Fleet, River 14
Fletcher, Geoffrey 8
Foster, Norman 16
Four Weddings and A Funeral 22
Foxe, John 46
Franklin, Benjamin 22
Friends of the City Churches 9
Frobisher, Martin 46
Fruiterers' Company 64
Fuke, Christopher 9

Garvin, JL 38
Gayer, Sir John 52
Geddes, Andrew 50
George II 76
George VI 40
Gibbons, Grinling 10, 64
Gibbs, James 10, 24
Gilbert Scott, Sir George 76
Gladstone, William 36
Gold, Henry 66
Goldsmiths' Company 90
Gould, James 32
Grant, Elizabeth 46
Gray, Thomas 76
Great Fire of London 7, 10, 12, 14, 18,
20, 26, 28, 30, 32, 34, 36, 38, 40, 42, 44,
46, 50, 54, 56, 58, 60, 62, 64, 66, 68, 70,
74, 76, 78, 80, 82, 84, 86, 90
Greenbelt 7, 12
Gresham College 48, 54
Gresham, Sir Thomas 48, 54
Guild of All Souls 52

Haakon VII 82
Hacker, Col Francis 80
Handel, George 14
Hardwick, Thomas 24
Hatton, Sir Christopher 14
Hawksmoor, Nicholas 8, 42, 50, 74,

76, 88
Hayes, Richard 74
Haymarket Theatre 26
Hays, Charles Melville 42
Hayward, John 68, 78
Hazlitt, William 14
Heming, John 66
Henry I 12
Henry III 40
Henry VIII 16, 24, 30, 70
Herrick, Robert 90
Hewitt, Garth 12
Hogarth, Paul 8
Hogarth, William 14, 22
Holbein, Hans 16
Holy Sepulchre 32
Hooke, Robert 7, 20, 42, 58, 62
Hope, Archbishop David 6, 7
Howells, Herbert 58
Huelin, Gordon 60
Hudson, Henry 44
Hunt, Holman 46

Industrial Christian Fellowship 52
Ingram AJ 58
Ingram HC 58
Innholders' Company 66
Ironmongers' Company 28
Irene, Princess 40

James I 18
James II 60, 64
Jeffreys, Judge George 10
Jenkins, Simon 6, 64
Jones, Inigo 24, 26
Juliana, Queen 40

Katharine of Aragon 16
Keats, John 32
Kempster, Christopher 64
Kempster, William 64
Kennet, Lord & Lady 9
King, Laurence 68
Kirk-Duncan, Brian 70
Knollys, Sir Francis 12

Lamb, Charles 14, 86
Laud, Archbishop William 52
Larke, Bl John 44
Lea-Cox, Peter 20
Leech, Kenneth 30
Limpus, Richard 76
Lion Sermon 52
Liverpool Street Station 12
Lloyd, Edward 74
Lloyd's 76
Lloyd's Choir 52
Lloyd's German Club 52
London, Archdeacon of 10
London Centre for Spirituality 42
London Transport 52

McCulloch, Joseph 68
McDonald, Trevor 68
Mansion House 88
Maratti, Carlo 60
Marsden, William 14
Matilda, Queen 12
Mendelssohn, Felix 58, 84
Merchant Taylors' Company 16
Milton, John 34, 46, 66
Mission to Seafarers 7, 78
Moore, Henry 88
Morris, Marcus 88
Mothersole, John 66
Mottistone, Lord 10
Much Hadham, Herts 88
Mullen, Peter 86
Munich 42

National Interpreting Service 36
New, Keith 80
Newton, John 74
Northcliffe, Lord 38
Norwood Cemetery 70

Observer, The 38
Old Bailey 62, 86

Palumbo, Lord 88
Parker, Archbishop William 64
Paul, Joanna 90

Penn, Admiral William 10, 62, 82
Penn, William 10
Pennsylvania 10
Pepys, Samuel 10, 34, 38, 82
Pepys Commemoration Service 82
Pewterers' Company 90
Philip, Admiral Arthur 68
Philip, Prince 78, 82
Pindar, Sir Paul 32
Place Below 68
Plaisterers' Company 28
Players of St Peter 36
Pocahontas, Princess 62, 86
Pope, Alexander 44
Popplewell, Richard 76
Prayer Book Society 50
Princess Royal 78
Pryse-Hawkins, Alfred 26
Puddle Dock 18
Purcell, Henry 52
Purchas, Samuel 62

Rahere 22, 24
Ramsey, Archbishop Michael 38
Rennert Jonathan 76
Rigg, Diana 68
Rodwell, JM 44
Rome 6, 12, 22
Rotherham, Archbishop Thomas 90
Rothermere, Lord 38
Rowlands Ingram, W 58
Royal College of Organists 14, 76
Royal Free Hospital 14
Rumens, Katharine 46

Saddlers' Company 90
St Alban Wood Street 90
St Alban's Holborn 78
St Bartholomew's Hospital 22, 86
St Bartholomew Moor Lane 42
St Christopher-le-Stocks 58, 90
St Erkenwald 44
St Etheldreda's Ely Place 26
St Gervais Paris 14
St James Duke's Place 52
St James the Great 10, 50

St John Fisher 10
St John the Baptist Brighton 72
St John Zachary 90
St John's Smith Square 18
St Leonard Foster Lane 28
St Martin Outwich 48
St Mary Magdalen Old Fish Street 62
St Mary Staining 90
St Martin Orgar 36
St Matthew Friday Street 90
St Michael-le-Querne 90
St Michael Queenhythe 50
St Michael Wood Street 20
St Mildred Bread Street 20
St Olave Old Jewry 58
St Olave Silver Street 90
St Patrick's Soho 72
St Paul's Cathedral 42, 64, 84, 88
St Peter Cheap 90
St Roche 10
St Swithin's London Stone 10
St Thomas Becket Chapel 56
St Thomas More 44, 54
St Thomas Syrian Orthodox Church 68
St Vincent Island 62
St Woolos Cathedral 26
Salters' Company 66
Samaritans 88
San Bartolomeo, Rome 22
Santa Maria della Concezione, Rome 12
Savage, Edwin 22
Schou, Carl 82
Shakespeare, William 26, 32, 46, 86
Shaw, Bernard 80
Sherrin, George 72
Shuttleworth, Henry 80
Simon the Anker 12
Sion College 38
Sisson, Marshall 18
Sir John Cass's Foundation 30
Skinners' Company 50
Smith, Capt John 86
Smith, Roland 44
Society of King Charles the Martyr 18

Somerset House 88
Southwark Cathedral 46, 64
Stationers' Company 34
Stock, Victor 68
Stone, JS 12
Stone, Nicholas 16
Stow, John 16
Strafford, Earl of 38
Stock Exchange 76
Studdert-Kennedy, Geoffrey 42

Tallow Chandlers' Company 54
Tanner, Alan 32
Tatchell, Rodney 30
Tathwell, Lincs 90
Telegraph, The Daily 34
Templeman Report 6, 7
Terry, Quinlan 48
Throkmorton, Sir Nicholas 52
Tillotson, Archbishop John 54
Times, The 44
Titanic 42
Toc H 10
Townend, Richard 58
Travers, Martin 56
Trinity Wall Street 68
Tyler, Wat 40
Tyndale, William 38, 86

Ursell, Philip 6

Vanbrugh, Sir John 74
Van Gogh, Vincent 40
Varah, Chad 88
Venice 6
Vintners' Company 50, 66
Virginia 86
Vitruvius, Pollio 74

Wagner, Sir Anthony 26
Wagstaffe, Thomas 60
Wallbank, Newall 22
Waltham, Abbot of 70
Walton, Izaak 38
Watts, GF 28
Wax Chandlers' Company 54

Webb, Sir Aston 22
Wesley, John 20
Westminster Cathedral 30, 72
Westminster Abbey 48, 56, 66
White, Thomas 38
Whittaker, Helen 44
Whittington, Richard 68, 78
Wilberforce, William 74
Wilhelmina, Queen 40
William I 28, 56
William III 16, 40, 60
Winchester, Marquess of 40
Wine & Spirit Trade Vintage Harvest
Festival 82
Wiseman, Cardinal Nicholas 72
Wood, Sir Henry 86
Wren, Sir Christopher 7, 14, 18, 20, 26,
30, 34, 36, 42, 50, 54, 56, 58, 60, 62, 64,
66, 68, 70, 76, 78, 80, 84, 86, 88, 90
Wyseman, Sir Robert 26